Like A Mighty Army

Acts 13:1—28:31

by Abe C. Van Der Puy
Voice of Missions
Back to the Bible

D1384200

Back to the Bible

Lincoln, Nebraska 68501

45,000 printed to date—1988
(5-5963—45M—68)
ISBN 0-8474-0716-0

Printed in the United States of America

Dedication

To our esteemed co-workers
at Back to the Bible and
HCJB/World Radio,
many of whom exhibit the
same qualities and commitment as
the Spirit-filled believers in Acts.

Introduction

In the first two volumes of this commentary on Acts, we considered *The Church Enlisted* (1:1—8:4) and *The Church Equipped* (8:5—12:25). In this third volume we'll observe the marvelous outreach of the early church—*The Church Extended* (13:1—28:31). Previously, I had divided the second half of Acts into "The Church Commissioned" (13:1—20:38) and "The Church Reinforced" (21:1—28:31). However, it will save time and space to combine these two into one grouping that we will call *The Church Extended.*

The last half of Acts deals with the great missionary journeys out from the church at Antioch. I have been revitalized in my own heart and ministry by joining Paul and Barnabas, as well as Silas and Luke, on these missionary trips. I recommend that you consult a good map of the areas involved. That will give you an excellent overview of where these fervent messengers went as they carried the Gospel of Jesus Christ to people in the then-known world.

Several important truths impressed me as I studied this inspiring story. First, in the work of the Lord, we continually encounter the contrast of "open doors and many adversaries," of opportunities and opposition, of triumphs and trials. We have a tendency to become discouraged when we confront adversaries, opposition and trials. We are tempted to think that such problems signify we are doing something wrong. But that is not the truth. Consequently, we should "keep on keeping on" when difficulties arise, trust the Lord and watch Him work in spite of opposition.

Second, the Lord provides His cheer and resources just when we need them. Paul's ministry illustrates this truth very clearly. In Corinth, in Jerusalem and on board the ship in the storm, God stood by Paul and provided the needed support. He will do the same for us as we seek to serve Him, especially as we labor to take His Gospel to everyone everywhere.

Third, although the men and women in Acts accomplished much as they spread the Gospel, we should remember that they were not supermen and superwomen. They had the same nature, feelings and weaknesses we do. We see many evidences of this in the second half of Acts. Paul and Barnabas had a strong argument concerning John Mark. They parted as a result and went their separate ways. These Gospel messengers also had problems at times with guidance, just as we sometimes do. They tried to go first to Asia, then to Bithynia and were finally led to Macedonia. Sometimes the Spirit-filled believers in the early church had great differences of opinion. One illustration is the big assembly in Jerusalem, described in Acts 15. But, praise God, they found the Spirit's answer. The great lesson for us is that God can work through our human weaknesses to do great and mighty things.

As J. A. Bengel has summarized the Book of Acts: "The victory of the word of God: Paul at Rome, the culmination of the gospel, the conclusion of Acts. . . . It began at Jerusalem; it finishes at Rome. Here, O church, thou hast thy pattern; it is thy duty to keep it, and to guard thy deposit" (quoted by F. F. Bruce, *The Book of the Acts*, pp. 535,536).

...plication of the gospel [...] Corinthians and Asia Tim-
...isem of Jerusalem is relative to Rome (Here, O
...church, that had the perfect [...] the day to keep it
...and to preach the gospel" translated by F. Rhodes. Her-
...London: ACLS pp. 33c.

Contents

Chapter   **Page**

1. Beginning the First Missionary Journey
   (13:1-52) 11

2. Completing the First Missionary Journey
   (14:1-28) 22

3. Making the Right Decision—With the Holy Spirit
   (15:1-35) 32

4. The Second Journey: Reaching New Areas
   (15:36—16:40) 41

5. The Second Journey: Evangelizing in Macedonia
   and Achaia (17:1—18:22) 53

6. The Third Journey: God's Word Growing Mightily
   in Ephesus (18:23—19:41) 65

7. The Third Journey: Continuing the Course
   (20:1-38) 79

8. The Third Journey: Making Difficult Choices
   (21:1-40) 90

9. Paul's Good Defense (22:1—23:11) 100

10. God Leads His Dear Servant Along
    (23:12—24:27) 108

11. Paul's Good Confession (25:1—26:32) 117

12. On the Way to Rome (27:1—28:10) 125

13. Bearing Witness at Rome (28:11-31) 133

Chapter 1

Beginning the First Missionary Journey
(Acts 13:1-52)

The Book of Acts has three broad divisions. First, the Jewish period of the church's witness (chs. 1-7). Second, the transition time from Jew to Gentile (chs. 8-12). Third, the Gentile phase of the church's outreach (chs. 13-28).

We can express these divisions in another way: the *founding* of the church, the *preparing* of the church, and the *extension* of the church. I have called these three periods: the church *enlisted*, the church *equipped*, and the church *extended*.

In this book we begin with Acts 13, which lets us see how the missionary journeys to the Gentiles began.

The Holy Spirit—the Missions Director

When we read Acts 13:1-3, it becomes clear that the missionary journeys arose from the Holy Spirit's initiative. However, He worked through willing and devoted leaders who received help from a cooperative congregation in Antioch.

The Spirit's Initiative

The great missionary outreach from Antioch began through the directive of the Holy Spirit, who said,

"Separate to Me Barnabas and Saul for the work to which I have called them" (Acts 13:2). We can, therefore, say that the Holy Spirit was the Missions Director of the Antioch church.

The question arises, "How did the Holy Spirit make His will known?" The Bible doesn't tell us specifically. Do you wonder why? I believe God didn't want us to become attached to one method of guidance. He often works in different ways. In this case maybe one of the five leaders became His spokesman. Or perhaps all five men received the same overpowering conviction at the same time.

We can have the assurance that the Holy Spirit still guides today. He doesn't always work dramatically. Most often He leads us quietly. But He always directs us surely and certainly if we are willing to follow. Think of the great promise in Psalm 37:23: "The steps of a good man are ordered by the Lord, and He delights in his way."

My wife and I often talk with our grown children and their spouses about the Holy Spirit's guidance. Recently one of the couples was facing some difficult decisions. At an especially crucial time, our son said, "Dad, Mom, right now I'd love to see a scroll come down out of heaven, telling me exactly what to do. But that isn't happening. I know, however, that by the Word of God and by the circumstances surrounding us, we can trust the Holy Spirit in us to help us make the proper choice." He was right. Sometimes the way doesn't seem completely clear, but afterwards we can truly appreciate all the way that the Lord has led us (see Deut. 8:2).

Today, just as He was back then, the Holy Spirit must be our Missions Director. If He is, then we will be successful in reaching out to new peoples and places with the Gospel. We often fail in this enterprise because we try to do it alone. If, as individuals and as churches, we want to be effectively involved in world-wide missions, then we must get our direction from the Holy Spirit as our CEO (Chief Executive Officer).

The Leaders' Devotion

The Holy Spirit doesn't work in a vacuum. He will not use unwilling or disobedient people. It's possible to quench and to grieve the Holy Spirit so much that we cannot hear His voice. The leaders in Antioch had a beautifully positive attitude toward the Holy Spirit. They desired to hear His voice and to obey. The Holy Spirit called His servants as they *praised, prayed* and *fasted.* He will do the same for us today as we make ourselves available to Him.

Look at the church leaders in Antioch. They represented a great variety of backgrounds. First, we find *Barnabas,* a Levite from Cyprus. Then *Simeon,* called Niger (which means "black" or "swarthy"). Perhaps he was the same person who carried Jesus' cross (see Luke 23:26). *Lucius* of Cyrene was one of the five. He came from North Africa. No doubt he, too, had dark skin. *Manaen* was included in the group. He had been raised with Herod, the tetrarch, so he grew up in a royal atmosphere. But Herod Antipas was also the person who ordered the beheading of John the Baptist. Last but not least, *Saul,* the Pharisee from Tarsus, belonged to this corps of leaders.

13

Though very diverse, these men demonstrated a beautiful unity. They had become one in Christ Jesus. The Gospel had given them a common goal. They loved the Lord Jesus; consequently, they loved each other. "Where there is neither Greek nor Jew, circumcised nor uncircumcised, barbarian, Scythian, slave nor free, but Christ is all and in all" (Col. 3:11). When Christian servants are *available* and *united* through the Holy Spirit, great things will happen in world evangelism.

The Church's Cooperation

Most Bible students believe that Acts 13:3 describes an action by the whole church. The members joined in prayer and fasting. They consecrated Saul and Barnabas to God's new call.

The phrase "they sent them away" can best be translated "they let them go" or "they released them." God had called Saul and Barnabas. The people of Antioch were, therefore, willing to let them go. Those who stayed behind made this sacrifice joyfully. God blesses abundantly when Christian congregations operate this way. On the other hand, churches become sterile and stagnant when they try to keep people and resources just for themselves. Jesus spoke truly when He said that when we try to save our lives for ourselves, we lose them. But when we lose them for Jesus' sake and the Gospel's, we find them (Mark 8:35).

We have just seen how dynamic missionary outreach happens. A group of Christians hear the Holy Spirit's call because they are in the right spiritual position to listen. Others in the fellowship cooperate fully in carrying out God's clear directive. That's how it works.

From this passage we can also gather important qualifications for a missionary. Saul and Barnabas had these qualities.

1. Tested and fruitful in home ministry
2. Diligent and self-denying in God's service
3. Called and sent by the Holy Spirit
4. Commissioned by a local church group
   This group stands behind the missionary. The missionary, in turn, is responsible to them.

Triumph of Spirit Power Over Evil

The Holy Spirit *called, sent* and *empowered*. We'll quickly see how necessary God's power was. Barnabas and Saul went first to the seaport of Antioch—Seleucia. Then they took a ship to Cyprus, which was about 60 miles away. No doubt they chose Cyprus as their first stop because it was Barnabas's home area (see Acts 4:36).

First, Barnabas and Saul preached the Word of God in Salamis (13:5). They witnessed primarily to Jews. Then, after touching other areas with the Gospel witness, they finally reached the other side of the island at Paphos (v. 6). There they first encountered the forces of evil.

In Paphos they met the governor of Cyprus, Sergius Paulus. He was an intelligent man (v. 7). Furthermore, he desired to hear the Word of God. How wonderful! Saul (now called Paul) and Barnabas had come to Cyprus for that very purpose.

But both the preachers and the interested hearer confronted a dangerous obstacle. The governor had employed an advisor by the name of Bar-Jesus, also called Elymas. He was a wayward Jew. He opposed Paul and Barnabas and tried to steer the governor away from faith (v. 8).

The Bible tells us that Paul was filled with the Holy Spirit (v. 9). I believe that means the Holy Spirit *especially empowered* him for this encounter. Note what he did. First, he rebuked Bar-Jesus very strongly. Second, he indicated that Bar-Jesus would be blind for a time, and it happened just as he predicted.

Today, just as it occurred in Paphos, the servants of Christ must meet the powers of darkness with God's power. I'm thankful for the times when I have seen valiant Christian witnesses rebuke Satan in Jesus' name—and Jesus' power has prevailed. Often I, too, have called on God's resources when it looked as though Satan's cohorts were gaining the upper hand. Then I watched the Holy Spirit turn the situation completely around. The lesson is clear—when God calls us and sends us, He also promises to empower us.

As a result of these events, Sergius Paulus believed. He was astonished at the teaching of the Lord (v. 12). We should never doubt God's power, especially the power of His living Word.

Before leaving this section, we should note two additional, significant items. First, we learn that John Mark had joined Barnabas and Paul as their assistant (v. 5). He was a nephew of Barnabas. We'll hear more about him later. Certainly, traveling and serving with Barnabas and Paul was a great opportunity for him.

Second, we learn that Saul's name was changed to Paul (v. 9). This represented a switch from his Jewish name to his Roman name. This seems very appropriate, because Paul would primarily minister to the Gentile world. He was ready to make every possible adaptation to best fit him for his God-appointed work. He later wrote: "I have become all things to all men, that I might by all means save some" (I Cor. 9:22). May God help us to follow his example!

Forward in Spite of Difficulties

Having completed their service in Cyprus, Paul, Barnabas and John Mark traveled to Perga by ship—a distance of more than 150 miles. It's significant to note how Luke, the author of Acts, now refers to the missionary party. Formerly, he spoke of them as Barnabas and Saul. Now he says, "Paul and his party" (Acts 13:13). This change signals the fact that Paul has become the leader of the missionary team, probably by direction of the Holy Spirit. We see no indication that Barnabas became jealous or upset. Other references to him in Acts let us know that he did not seek status or recognition. He just wanted to serve and didn't worry about who got the credit.

John Mark Leaves the Team

We don't know exactly why John Mark left Paul and Barnabas. Some think that the trip was proving too rigorous for the young man. Others speculate that he was unhappy when the leadership passed to Paul, especially since he was related to Barnabas. Still other commentators have surmised that John Mark didn't agree with Paul's change of emphasis in turning to the Gentiles with the Gospel.

We only know that John Mark left. Later, Paul and Barnabas would have an argument over John Mark that would separate them (see Acts 15:36-41). But eventually Paul would recognize him as a useful servant (II Tim. 4:11).

I like to think of John Mark as "The Failure Who Made Good." His story should encourage us, especially if we feel we abandoned ship when we should have carried out a promised commitment.

The departure of John Mark must have tempted Paul and Barnabas to be discouraged. But with God's power they went on. Do we?

Illness in Perga

Perga was a lowland city. Consequently, malaria was a threat. Paul must have become very ill in Perga, so he left Perga and went on to Galatia. He refers to this in Galatians 4:13: "You know that because of physical infirmity I preached the gospel to you at the first."

Paul and Barnabas could have concluded that this illness would be a good reason for not completing their missionary journey. But did they quit? No, they just switched to Plan B. That's what good missionaries do.

A Difficult Journey to Pisidian Antioch

Pisidian Antioch lay 100 miles from Perga over a rough road that included a mountain pass. Robbers and brigands made the road dangerous. Paul was probably thinking about this trip when he wrote in II Corinthians 11:26: "in journeys often . . . in perils of robbers." But even so they went. The message had to be preached, even though they suffered illness and faced a long, hard trip.

Gospel Preaching and Its Results

Paul received an invitation to preach in the synagogue in Pisidian Antioch (Acts 13:14-16). Two groups of people were gathered in the synagogue. First, pure Jews who were following the teachings of the Old Testament. Second, non-Jews who had become adherents to the Jewish faith. That's why Paul addressed them in verse 16 as "men of Israel" (group 1) and "you who fear God" (group 2).

Paul's Message

First, Paul reminded them of the history of God's dealings with the people of Israel, starting in the land of Egypt and going through the time of King David. Then, he made it clear that Jesus had come from the line of David in fulfillment of prophecy. He suffered death on the cross, but He also rose from the dead and was seen by many witnesses. Paul made a distinction between David, the great king, who died and did not rise, and the Lord Jesus, the greater King, who died and rose again. He told the people that through this Lord Jesus Christ they could have forgiveness of sins and be justified. But this justification comes to those who believe. If they did not believe, they would face the

19

serious consequences of unbelief. The same is true for us today.

A Good Response

The Gentiles, and even some Jews, rejoiced in the message. Paul and Barnabas urged them to continue in the grace of God.

On the second Sabbath, almost the entire city came to hear God's Word. However, the legalistic Jews didn't like it at all. They were filled with envy as they saw the interested multitudes. (By contrast, Jesus was filled with compassion when He saw the multitudes.) Jealousy in spiritual matters is an awful thing. The elder brother was jealous when he became angry instead of joyful upon seeing his prodigal brother finally come home (see Luke 15:11-32).

The legalistic Jews opposed Paul, "contradicting and blaspheming" (Acts 13:45). So Paul said, in essence, "We wanted to give you the Gospel first. But since you reject it, we will turn to the Gentiles" (v. 46).

This action by Paul inspired and gladdened the Gentiles. Many of them believed. As a result, the Word of God spread throughout the entire region. The spreading of God's Word has continued through the centuries and is still taking place today.

Frequently in our missionary service we have seen large, rejoicing crowds of men and women who were recently converted to Christ. I remember one scene in particular. About 3000 mountain Indians, descendants of the Incas, had gathered together. They were celebrating the completion of the translation and printing of the Bible in their language. They covered a large hillside, dressed in their colorful ponchos and their embroidered blouses. Their faces were shining brightly because they had the joy of salvation in Christ.

Violent Opposition

In Pisidian Antioch the jealous and legalistic Jews stirred up the prominent people of the area. They expelled Paul and Barnabas from their city. But these intrepid missionaries just shook the dust off their feet (as the Lord had instructed His disciples to do in Matt. 10:14,15) and went on to Iconium. Once more we see that the Gospel divides. The preaching of the Gospel often arouses persecution. But, thank the Lord, it also brings salvation to those who believe.

Joy—the Accompaniment of True Evangelism

Acts 13:52 declares, "And the disciples were filled with joy and with the Holy Spirit." Bible scholars differ in their interpretation of who is meant by the word "disciples"—Paul and Barnabas or the new believers in that region. I think we can apply the description to both groups. Both those who share the Gospel and those who receive it know joy and the Holy Spirit's power. That's the way the story of true evangelism always ends.

Chapter 2

Completing the First Missionary Journey
(Acts 14:1-28)

Acts 14 presents some remarkable actions and events: 1) It tells about powerful evangelism in Iconium, Lystra and Derbe; 2) it gives us a picture of Christian courage in the midst of opposition; 3) it shows us how careful the apostles were to give glory to God; 4) it permits us to see how diligent these Christian missionaries were in follow-up work; and 5) it recounts the story of the great meeting that occurred in Antioch when Paul and Barnabas returned.

Blessing in Iconium in Spite of Opposition

Iconium was located about 100 miles southeast of Pisidian Antioch. Paul and Barnabas again preached in a synagogue. They "so spoke that a great multitude . . . believed" (Acts 14:1). We realize that power doesn't reside in the messenger but in the Word of God. Nevertheless, God works through human instruments genuinely yielded to Him.

How did Paul and Barnabas speak? No doubt it was similar to the way Paul preached to the Corinthians: "My speech and my preaching were not with persuasive words of human wisdom, but in demonstration of the Spirit and of power, that your faith should not be in the wisdom of men but in the power of God" (I Cor. 2:4,5). We can also work and witness this way. And when we do, we can expect God's blessing.

Again, the sharing of the Gospel brought strong opposition. The Scriptures use very strong language to describe the reaction. Acts 14:2 says, "But the unbelieving Jews stirred up the Gentiles and poisoned their minds against the brethren." Verse 4 adds, "But the multitude of the city was divided: part sided with the Jews, and part with the apostles."

When we share the Gospel, we can expect Satan's counterattack. Opposition should not surprise us. Remember the prophetic words of the Lord: "Do you suppose that I came to give peace on earth? I tell you, not at all, but rather division" (Luke 12:51). We should not become discouraged when opposition arises. Paul said at one point in his ministry, "For a great and effective door has opened to me, and there are many adversaries" (I Cor. 16:9). *Opportunities* and *opposition* often occur at the same time.

Once again, the danger didn't cause the missionary team to quit. Instead, "they stayed there a long time, speaking boldly in the Lord" (Acts 14:3). Here we observe the courage and dedication of these servants of the Lord. They could have tried to find a more convenient and hospitable place for witness. But they didn't do that, because they felt God wanted them in Iconium. They knew that the safest location was in the will of God.

Paul and Barnabas also showed that they did know when to leave. When their opponents became violent

23

in plotting to harm them, they decided the time had come to leave (vv. 5,6). They had two reasons for this course of action. First, they had done their assigned work in Iconium. Second, they didn't want to be foolhardy. They believed it right to exercise reasonable caution. So they went on to Lystra and Derbe. Lystra lay about 18 miles slightly southwest, and Derbe was about 20 miles southeast of Lystra.

Giving Glory to God in Lystra

Things moved quickly in Lystra. A cripple who had never walked listened with great interest to Paul's preaching. Paul noticed how intently he was following the message and realized he had faith. So he commanded him to stand up. The lame man responded and experienced healing. The Lord had worked a miracle through Paul in response to the man's faith.

When this happened, the crowd began to worship Paul and Barnabas. The people believed that the gods had come down in human form. They called Barnabas Zeus—probably because of his dignified appearance. They labeled Paul Hermes because he did most of the speaking. Then the multitude, led by the priest of the temple of Zeus, prepared to offer a sacrifice to Paul and Barnabas.

Among primitive peoples you find many legends and stories about gods taking on human form. I think this provides evidence of a universal longing for a personal God. This longing found fulfillment in Jesus Christ, who "became flesh and dwelt among us" (John 1:14).

When Paul and Barnabas realized what was happening, they were horrified. They tore their clothes in

24

dismay. Quickly they tried to convince the people that they were human beings—no different from them. Paul and Barnabas did not want any glory for themselves, because all the glory belonged to the Lord. Like John the Baptist, they were declaring by word and deed: "He must increase, but I must decrease" (3:30). We all need to learn this lesson—not I but Christ.

As he often did, Paul turned this situation into an occasion to preach (Acts 14:15-17). Notice how beautifully he adapted his presentation. The people had very little Old Testament background. Therefore, he didn't speak to them as he had to those in Pisidian Antioch. He talked about God, the Creator. He emphasized God's patience with disobedient people. He mentioned some signs of God's goodness—that He sent rain from heaven and gave fruitful seasons, which brought food and gladness. I'm sure that, after this introduction, Paul became much more specific about the Gospel. We know some must have trusted Christ, because later verses tell us that Paul and Barnabas returned to encourage the believers and appoint elders (see vv. 21-23). Even after Paul had delivered his powerful message, many of the people still wanted to sacrifice to him and Barnabas.

This dramatic story contains some great lessons for us. First, we need to give glory to God instead of taking the glory for ourselves. Second, we should learn to faithfully preach the Gospel, even in very difficult circumstances. Third, we should be willing to adapt our approach to people who have very little basic knowledge of Christian truth. We should, of course, never change the heart of the message. But we should be willing to change our methods and procedures to fit the situation. Again I am reminded of what Paul said in I Corinthians 9:22: "I have become all things to all men, that I might by all means save some."

Suffering Triumphantly for Jesus' Sake

While Paul and Barnabas were actively ministering, unbelieving Jews came all the way from Antioch and Iconium to incite the people (Acts 14:19). They persuaded the multitude to turn against Paul and Barnabas. Their wrath boiled over against Paul especially. As a consequence, the same folks who had earlier sought to worship the missionaries now stoned Paul right inside the city. When they thought he was dead, they dragged him outside the city limits.

What an experience that must have been for Paul! Of course, he had never forgotten the impact of seeing Stephen stoned (7:54-60). Now he was going through the same suffering. Paul spoke about this later in II Corinthians 11:25: "Once I was stoned." The trial was a great one, not soon forgotten.

But Paul didn't die. This could have resulted from a miracle touch of God upon him. Paul revived while faithful disciples gathered around him (Acts 14:20). It must have taken a lot of trust in God for these new believers to identify with the missionaries as they did.

It's possible that a young man named Timothy was in that group. He is mentioned in Acts 16:1,2. Timothy, of course, became a great helper to Paul, as well as an effective servant of the Lord Jesus. The stoning of Paul and Paul's response to it would have made a deep impression on Timothy.

26

Later in his life, Paul spoke about the persecution he suffered in Antioch, Iconium and Lystra. "Persecutions, afflictions, which happened to me at Antioch, at Iconium, at Lystra—what persecutions I endured. And out of them all the Lord delivered me" (II Tim. 3:11). In Antioch and Iconium God kept Paul from being stoned. In Lystra God delivered Paul even through stoning. Many of us have had similar experiences. In some cases the Lord has prevented severe trials from coming upon us. In other situations He has given us the ability to be victorious in trials. Hebrews 11 explains clearly how God saves His people *out of* difficulty and *in* difficulty through faith.

Notice the courage and perseverance of Paul, as well as of the others who accompanied him. First, after regaining consciousness (or perhaps even coming back to life), Paul went back into Lystra. Why did he do that? I believe he felt it was God's will and that God could care for him there. Second, the next day Paul and Barnabas went on to Derbe, about 20 miles away. Many of us would not walk 20 miles if we were in good condition. But Paul did it the day after his enemies had almost stoned him to death. His actions speak volumes. They reveal the intensity of Paul's commitment to God.

Confirming the New Believers

After they had preached the Gospel in Derbe and made many disciples (Acts 14:21), the missionaries evidently felt that God was leading them to bring their first journey to a close. They could have traveled over a nearby mountain pass and arrived quite quickly at

27

Paul's home city of Tarsus. That would have been a tempting road of convenience after such a long and hard missionary journey. But Paul and Barnabas followed the line of dedication to duty. First, they felt a responsibility to visit the many new believers before returning to their home church. Second, they considered it important to report to the congregation and people who had sent them out.

Paul and Barnabas went right back to Lystra, Iconium and Antioch where they had encountered great difficulties. No doubt they felt God was leading them back and would protect them. Furthermore, their ministry this time was far less public than on their first visit.

It's instructive even today to examine their ministry with the new believers. Their work had a fourfold emphasis.

1. They urged their brothers and sisters to continue in the faith. They underlined the importance of perseverance.

2. They enunciated the principle, "We must through many tribulations enter the kingdom of God" (v. 22). They helped the converts realize that persecution is a sign of God's love and favor rather than a token of His wrath. *Places of suffering become places of power.* Adversaries will greatly test us. But we will find that God is greater than them all. Often the strongest believers have been strengthened through suffering.

3. They appointed elders in every church (v. 23). These elders had the responsibility for the leadership and government of the churches. The word that is

translated "appointed" can also have the meaning of "elected under the apostles' direction." These elders must have been relatively young believers. But Paul and Barnabas trusted the work of God in their lives, because they knew that the Holy Spirit works in the life of every obedient believer.

4. They exercised a dedication ministry (v. 23). They prayed and fasted with the new believers. Remember that this missionary journey began with prayer and fasting. That's how the work of God would continue. These new churches would begin their own missionary outreach. Here we find the secret of success in God's work today. Through prayer and fasting we worship God, we then hear Him speaking to us, and we go forth in His power and blessing.

Finally, Paul and Barnabas made their way home, no doubt very weary. But that didn't keep them from preaching the Gospel in Perga. Apparently they hadn't had that opportunity the first time through. I'm amazed and delighted at their wonderful dedication.

Reporting What God Had Done

We haven't been very aware of the sending church while the missionary journey was in progress. But the church was supporting Paul and Barnabas in prayer. The good things that happened on the trip resulted from the backing of the church. That's why they needed to report to the people. The same factors hold true today.

Paul and Barnabas rehearsed all that God had done with them (or through them). They had been God's

29

instruments, but God had done the work. It must have been wonderful to hear Paul and Barnabas tell what God had done. Their report of those who trusted Christ must have thrilled the congregation. It's the same today. I never tire of telling people in missionary conferences what God has done.

We must never forget—missionaries and churches alike—that it's God's work we are doing. Even when things look their blackest, God is in charge of the whole matter. We can, therefore, expect Him to triumph.

Paul and Barnabas also testified to God's opening the door of faith—not only for the Jews but also for the Gentiles. God will open the door of faith to all who will receive Christ. We know that as we share the Gospel message, the Word of God blessed by the Spirit of God does the work—people are brought to faith in Christ.

Many times my wife and I have presented the Gospel message. What a delight it has been to see people respond and trust the Saviour! Even simple and primitive peoples understand as God works in their lives. And, on the other end of the scale, highly educated men and women who find it difficult to believe, also come to faith in our Lord as our great God works through His Word.

We could also call this a time of furlough for Paul and Barnabas. They needed this time of *fellowship* and *rejuvenation*. They were strengthening their bonds with the local church. Their purpose in this was to prepare for the next chapter of missionary outreach that God had planned for them. In military parlance we call this R & R (Rest and Recreation). Spiritual warfare requires the same. We can serve God best when we discover a right balance between needed rest and dynamic action. A respected missionary colleague used to say to me, "Abe, we often need to retreat to go forward. We retrench to advance." More than anything else we need to remember, "Those who wait on the Lord shall renew their strength" (Isa. 40:31).

Chapter 3

Making the Right Decision—
With the Holy Spirit
(Acts 15:1-35)

Great blessings often bring with them problems and crises. Dynamic movements produced by God's power can result in growing pains. We can consider them good difficulties. They give evidence of life. If we are only looking for a peaceful place, we should go to a cemetery. It's peaceful there all right, but it's the peace of death.

The vigorous growth of the Antioch church and God's blessings on the first missionary journey brought many Gentiles into the Christian Church. Their coming raised big questions among Jewish believers. At this point, the Church needed Holy Spirit guidance to make the right decision. Acts 15 tells the story.

The Conflict

The principal problem arose out of this question: How much of the Jewish Law and ritual did the Gentiles have to observe to be genuine Christians and members of the Church? Some Jewish believers came from Jerusalem to Antioch, insisting that the Gentiles had to be circumcised and keep the Law of Moses in order to be saved. In other words, salvation was by grace through faith *plus* quite a few other Jewish rituals. If this viewpoint had won, Christianity would have remained a small Jewish sect or would have been divided into a Hebrew church and a Gentile church of Christ.

Paul and Barnabas opposed this viewpoint. They argued that the Gentiles didn't have to become Jews to be genuine Christians and members of the Church. This led to great dissension and dispute (Acts 15:2). I'm reminded of what Professor William LaSor wrote: "The more I study the Early Church the more I see it as a Spirit-led human institution, with the strengths of the Spirit and the weaknesses of human beings" (*Church Alive,* p. 236). I'd like to amend LaSor's statement by saying, "I see it as a Spirit-led *divine* institution—but with the obvious weaknesses of human beings."

The issue was so important that Paul and Barnabas and others were sent to Jerusalem to discuss the matter with the apostles and elders there. In time of need we can usually find good help in consultation with godly men and women.

We should not criticize the Judaizers too harshly. They sincerely resisted change, even though they were sincerely wrong. Some of them had faithfully kept the Jewish rules and traditions all their lives. Now they saw big changes coming.

Like them, many of us resist change. We find it hard to distinguish between fundamentals and incidentals, between principles and methods, between basic Bible truth and our own man-made traditions. When we

33

think about these people in the early church, we also need to remember that they didn't have the advantage of New Testament teaching, because the New Testament hadn't been written yet.

Let's think of specific examples to show the difference between eternal truth we must retain and methods or styles that can change. The doctrine of the deity of Christ will never change. By contrast, the order and style of a worship service can easily change without doing violence to a fundamental truth. The Bible also prescribes certain basic principles of government that are enduring, such as "Righteousness exalts a nation, but sin is a reproach to any people" (Prov. 14:34). But that same Bible does not set forth an ironclad political position. Within the parameters of righteousness, different forms of government can exist. The Bible also teaches clearly that all of us need to study its truths faithfully (see Ps. 119). Nevertheless, we have the liberty of choosing the form or method we will use for Bible study. The necessity of Bible study is an enduring principle. The method of Bible study can change.

The Conference

The church in Jerusalem took this matter seriously. The leaders made sure that they gave the question wide exposure. The narrative in Acts makes it clear that, not only the apostles and elders but also the church members were involved (15:4,22). The leaders gave the Judaizers, or the Pharisee group, opportunity to express their convictions. They didn't confine the

34

discussion to one side. They knew that each church member had a big stake in this discussion. They realized that all sincere believers have an important part to play in the life of the church. The story of the Jerusalem conference does not present the picture of a limited hierarchy imposing its will on others. Instead, we see participation by the members in seeking God's solution to the problem. Christians grow by thinking, discussing and praying about important matters as they search for God's answers.

Peter was at the conference along with Paul and Barnabas. Later, we see that James emerged as the guiding leader (v. 13).

The question at hand produced much dispute and discussion. Often we think of this as negative, but it doesn't have to be. It's possible to dispute and discuss a matter with love and frankness when you're looking for God's answers. Too often in our congregations problems are left to boil underneath the surface and remain unresolved. Such situations are not healthy. It's much better to face the problems frankly in a Christian spirit. This can cause some pain at first; but as believers work together to resolve the difficulty, it will end on a positive note.

The Pharisees argued that the Gentiles had to be circumcised and keep the Law of Moses to be saved (v. 5). Peter, however, answered by testifying about what God had done among the Gentiles. The Lord gave them His Holy Spirit when they believed (v. 8). He purified their hearts by faith (v. 9). God did this without their being circumcised or keeping the Law of Moses. Peter then made a very bold statement: "But we believe that through the grace of the Lord Jesus Christ we shall be saved in the same manner as they" (v. 11). *The Living Bible* paraphrases this sentence: "Don't you believe that all are saved the same way, by the free gift of the Lord Jesus?" In other words, Jew and Gentile alike are saved by believing in the Lord Jesus, not by observing rituals.

After Peter finished, the multitude was silent while Paul and Barnabas spoke about the miracles God had worked through them among the Gentiles—without circumcision or the keeping of Jewish ritual.

After listening to all of the arguments, James expressed his viewpoint. He said, in essence, "The testimony of Peter, Paul and Barnabas agrees with Scripture" (vv. 14,15). He quoted from Amos 9:11,12, which talks about God's purposes for all mankind. This passage even says that the Gentiles would be called by God's name (v. 12).

When we study how the Jerusalem conference proceeded, we see three ingredients. First, the people acknowledged the presence of the Holy Spirit. Second, they listened to testimony from the Lord's servants concerning how God had been working through their preaching and witnessing. Third, they looked to the Scriptures for guidance and confirmation on the issue. We can be assured of finding God's answers when these three factors serve as the foundation for our search.

The Conclusion

What the Jerusalem conference concluded was expressed by James and later was stated in the letter sent to the church at Antioch. Regarding salvation, they decided that they should not trouble the Gentiles with keeping Jewish ritual. It was enough for the Gentiles to turn to God through Jesus Christ. *Salvation was by grace through faith plus nothing.* That principle is as relevant today as it was when James enunciated it. The Gospel is a simple message; let's not complicate it by adding our own cultural baggage.

Even though nothing could be added to salvation, the Gentiles did need to exercise care in daily conduct. By doing this, they would strengthen their fellowship with all believers and give a clear testimony to unbelievers. The conference spoke specifically about three areas: having *consideration,* avoiding *compromise* and fleeing *corruption.*

Having Consideration

The Jerusalem conference urged the Gentiles not to eat blood or things strangled (from which the blood had not been drained). Here we need to remember Leviticus 17:11 and other related passages: "For the life of the flesh is in the blood." To eat blood would greatly offend Jewish believers. The Gentiles, therefore, were encouraged to refrain from this practice in consideration for their Jewish brothers and sisters.

We should have this same attitude today. Love for fellow Christians and a desire to honor God will give us sensitive spirits. We will want to avoid conduct that offends other believers, for we will not want to hurt them or put a stumbling block in their way (see Rom. 14:1-13).

Avoiding Compromise

The Gentiles were told to avoid eating meat offered to idols. Such eating could easily give the appearance of evil. The meat in question had been offered to idols in pagan temples. This meat would then be sold in the public market. It therefore had a bad association, for some felt that eating the meat was as bad as worshiping the idol. Paul later addressed this same issue in Romans 14:14-23 and I Corinthians 8.

The ruling of the Jerusalem Council teaches us that we should never do anything that will tend to compromise our testimony. Romans 14:23 says, "Whatever is not from faith is sin."

Fleeing Corruption

The third guideline established by the conference told the Gentiles to "abstain . . . from sexual immorality" (Acts 15:20). Such conduct was definitely wrong for Jew or Gentile. Every believer must flee iniquity and corruption. This is one of God's fundamental principles.

The conclusions reached at the Jerusalem conference set a standard that still applies today. We have a beautifully simple message to tell: Salvation is by grace through faith plus nothing. After salvation, the believer will live in consideration for others, avoid compromise and shun corruption.

Today, the godless philosophy that says, "If it feels good, do it" is invading the church. More than ever we need to combat such an attitude by teaching Christian consideration, by refusing to compromise in our conduct and by fleeing corruption. Then our pure lives and our loving service will bring great honor to our wonderful Lord.

The Communication

The whole church, along with the apostles and elders, agreed with what James said. They wrote in the letter: "It seemed good to the Holy Spirit, and to us" (Acts 15:28). They also wrote that they had assembled "with one accord" (v. 25). Even though they began with differing opinions and engaged in much discussion, they assembled with unity of spirit for a common purpose. Together they wanted to know and do God's will.

The letter they wrote to the church at Antioch breathes Christian love. In it they contrasted the Judaizers with Paul and Barnabas (vv. 24-26). The Judaizers had troubled the new believers with words (talk is cheap). But Paul and Barnabas had risked their lives to preach the Gospel and obey God. They concluded that it is better to listen to those who *practice* the Gospel rather than to those who just *talk* about it.

In this letter the Jerusalem conference stated clearly what James had announced earlier. They would not lay on the Gentiles the burden of Jewish rituals. The Gentiles just needed to keep on believing in Jesus.

The church in Jerusalem sent the letter by personal messengers. It's always better to deal with delicate and important matters in person rather than just in writing. The two go very well together—the letter and the personal visit.

The Confirmation

The appointed messengers, Judas and Silas, arrived in Antioch and delivered the letter (Acts 15:30). The multitude rejoiced. No doubt it was a beautiful scene.

Judas and Silas, being prophets, used the occasion to *exhort* the believers and to *encourage* them, just as the letter did. These two things go very well together in Christian ministry—exhortation and encouragement. We should use the pair much more than we do.

Paul and Barnabas continued their teaching and preaching ministry in Antioch. Times of crisis became occasions for growth. The same is true today. Together we learn more of the truth of God. We haven't finished the course when we come to Christ. We need to grow in Him through learning more of His truth and through communion with His people.

The church experienced a great victory by making the right decision. The believers unitedly sought God's will through the guidance of the Holy Spirit. If we meet the conditions as they did, we will also come to right conclusions. As a result, we will reach out farther and farther with the Gospel—as they did.

Chapter 4

The Second Journey: Reaching New Areas
(Acts 15:36—16:40)

Acts 15:36—16:40 relates the launching of the second missionary journey. It didn't occur without difficulties. But through them all, the Lord was guiding His servants. This passage also presents some great illustrations of the Gospel at work. When we see what God did in the lives of Lydia, the slave girl and the Philippian jailer, we can take courage in our witness today.

Receiving God's Guidance

The Holy Spirit often guides us in ordinary circumstances and in spite of our human weaknesses. We sometimes think that God can work only when we exhibit our best performance and when all the circumstances are right. However, God has chosen to carry out His purposes through frail human instruments—us. Because we are human, we often have to perform our ministries in contrary circumstances. Our Father knows this very well and "remembers that we are dust" (Ps. 103:14).

Even After a Bad Start

Acts 15:36-41 does not show Paul and Barnabas at their best. Certainly they exhibited real fervency in planning for another hard missionary journey. However, even before they started, they had a strong argument. Barnabas wanted to take John Mark with them. But Paul said, in essence, "Nothing doing."

We can understand why these men clashed. Paul, the man of great intensity, didn't want anyone along who wouldn't be wholehearted. Barnabas, with his kind spirit, saw an opportunity to help someone who had failed.

Both stood their ground. The argument became so heated that they parted company. We would think that these two good brothers could find a compromise. Barnabas was called the "Son of Encouragement" (4:36). Paul later wrote the great love chapter, I Corinthians 13. Couldn't such men settle their argument? Evidently not.

But God overruled this incident of human weakness. Two Gospel teams resulted. Paul chose Silas, and Barnabas took John Mark. We're tempted to ask, "Who was right?" The Bible doesn't give us a definite answer. The church evidently thought Paul was right because they commended him and Silas to the grace of God (Acts 15:40). However, later developments reveal that John Mark turned out OK. Paul testified, "He is useful to me for ministry" (II Tim. 4:11). Perhaps Paul's sternness spoke to John Mark about perseverance. Barnabas's kindness gave him the hope of making good.

With Provision of a New Helper

It must have encouraged Paul to meet Timothy in Derbe and Lystra. Right from the start this disciple

42

enjoyed a good reputation (Acts 16:1,2). He had a Jewish mother and a Greek father. Both his mother, Eunice, and his grandmother, Lois, demonstrated genuine faith (II Tim. 1:5). Many commentators presume that Timothy's father was not living when Paul came to Derbe and Lystra on this visit.

Timothy became a great stalwart in cooperation with Paul. He served as Paul's messenger (I Cor. 4:17). He accompanied Paul during his first imprisonment in Rome (Phil. 2:19). Paul called him a beloved son (I Cor. 4:17). In Philippians 2:20-22 Paul paid Timothy his greatest compliment: "For I have no one like-minded, who will sincerely care for your state. . . . But you know his proven character, that as a son with his father he served with me in the gospel."

Before leaving, Paul circumcised Timothy. This seems strange in view of Paul's strong statements against the Jewish practice in the opening verses of Galatians 5. However, in Galatians 5 Paul was speaking against those who were trying to impose Jewish rituals on newly converted Gentiles. Since Timothy was half Jewish, it was appropriate for him to be circumcised. Such a step would help him in his work with Jewish people and would not hinder him in his service with Gentiles.

Paul, Silas and Timothy were now ready to continue their mission. They carried with them a statement concerning the conclusions of the Jerusalem Council. They delivered these "decrees" to the churches. God also used the three men to strengthen the congregations, which then "increased in number daily" (Acts 16:5).

Paul and his company planned to go to Asia. That made good sense. But the Holy Spirit said, "No." He did not permit them to preach the Word in Asia (Acts 16:6).

Then they attempted to go into Bithynia. But the Spirit blocked their way again (v. 7). In such circumstances many of us would have said, "What is God trying to do with us? Maybe we shouldn't have started out on this journey." But the three Christian soldiers didn't have that attitude. They kept on trying—and finally came to Troas (v. 8).

In Troas they learned why the Lord had prevented them from going to Asia and Bithynia. He wanted them in Macedonia. In Troas the Lord spoke to Paul through a vision in which a man pleaded, "Come over to Macedonia and help us" (v. 9). Some Bible students believe that Luke was the man from Macedonia, because he joined the party at Troas. We know he joined them because he begins to use the word "we" in verse 10.

What response did Paul and his party give to this divine call? "Immediately we sought to go to Macedonia" (v. 10). It warms our hearts to see that kind of obedience.

We don't know the details of how God guided His servants—first negatively and then positively. We don't need that information. But we do know God still guides today by steps and stops (see Ps. 37:23,24).

Remember how God has directed you. Perhaps He kept you from having liberty when you began to do a certain thing. I vividly recall one instance of His guidance. It occurred in Ecuador, South America, at Missionary Radio Station HCJB. We were searching for a site for a new transmitter and antenna installation. We thought we had found several "ideal" places. But they all fell through. Then the Lord brought a landowner to us who offered to sell us some property. It turned out to be the right one. If we had succeeded in obtaining one of the other properties we so earnestly desired, we wouldn't have been able to develop hydroelectric power at a later date. The place God had chosen lay in a strategic spot for something we had not yet envisioned.

This passage speaks to us about God's guidance and missionary perseverance. Paul, Silas and Timothy could have doubted. But as William LaSor says, "Apostles are made of sterner stuff—at least, Paul was. Apostles say, 'If God doesn't want me here, He must want me there. If He wants me to be silent here, it must be for a good reason. If He doesn't want me to take Barnabas, He must have some other work for Barnabas, and He must have someone else to go along with me.'

"That is why God uses apostles" (*Church Alive,* p. 249).

Proving the Gospel's Power

The missionary journey was proceeding according to the will of God. Paul and his party were reaching into Europe, finally arriving at Philippi, one of the most important cities in Macedonia (Acts 16:12). They had obeyed God, and He promised to bless their ministry.

45

They carried the greatest message in the world—that Jesus came to save sinners who believe. We will see how powerful the Gospel is to change people of all classes and conditions.

Lydia—the Lady With the Open Heart and Home

The missionary team found Philippi to be very poor spiritually. The city had no synagogue. This meant that less than ten men in the city worshiped God according to Old Testament revelation.

But the spiritual poverty of Philippi didn't discourage the missionaries. It challenged them. They looked for openings to introduce the Gospel. They found one such opportunity at the riverside. Some devout women routinely went there to pray (Acts 16:13). It was a humble place to begin—at the river with just a handful of women (who weren't very important in the thinking of the average Jewish man). But Paul, Silas and Timothy didn't belittle the opportunity. They knew that God can work anywhere—among women and men alike.

They weren't disappointed. A lady from Thyatira by the name of Lydia demonstrated her interest (v. 14). She sold garments dyed purple, which were very much in demand as well as very costly. She obviously had abundant resources or she could not have provided the hospitality she did (v. 15). God opened Lydia's heart and that of her household. They were the first recorded converts in Europe. No doubt Paul, Silas and Timothy rejoiced in this great breakthrough.

As soon as Lydia believed, she opened her home to the Gospel workers. She didn't do it perfunctorily. She constrained them to accept her hospitality—she insisted on it. This suggests that the missionaries were reluctant to accept her offer at first. But when they saw the obvious work of God in her life as well as her Christian love, they accepted her offer.

The Bible consistently tells us to provide hospitality to others. In our depersonalized society we can easily neglect it. That's a mistake. Like Lydia, we should be hospitable.

The Slave Girl Freed From Satan's Power

Next, the missionary team met a slave girl (Acts 16:16). She was possessed by at least one of Satan's demons. Her unscrupulous masters used that to their financial advantage. Through the demon's help, she had an ability in fortune-telling. Many customers paid for her services. The world hasn't changed. People still profit today from the misfortune of others and from sinful deeds. Think of the miserable men and women who are making millions through pornography and trafficking in drugs.

The girl followed the missionaries, crying out, "These men are the servants of the Most High God, who proclaim to us the way of salvation" (v. 17). Notice that she spoke the truth. She did this for many days.

What did Paul say, "Thanks for the free advertising"? No, he was greatly annoyed. First, he objected to the way the slave girl was being misused. Second, no matter how cooperative the Devil may seem to be, he is still our enemy. We should never make any kind of alliance with him. He tries to defeat us by alliance (as an

47

angel of light) or by antagonism. The first is more dangerous.

Paul won a great victory in Jesus' name. He commanded the demon to come out of the girl, and she was freed (v. 18). The Bible doesn't specifically say she was converted, but I like to think that she took the step of faith. Thank God for His power! Are we ready to use it by faith today?

This good deed brought suffering to the missionaries. The girl's masters reacted because they had lost their financial gain. They incited a multitude. The magistrates, who should have maintained order, joined in the persecution (v. 22). They tore the clothes off Paul and Silas and gave the order to beat them. Then they turned the wounded men over to the jailer. He threw them into the worst part of the prison and added insult to injury by putting them into stocks. In that miserable condition they spent the night. They suffered imprisonment because a slave girl had been liberated from Satan's clutches. How often people pervert justice. The authorities should have applauded Paul and Silas instead of punishing them.

The Jailer—Saved With His Whole Household

The salvation of the jailer was preceded by two great phenomena—the singing of Paul and Silas and a great earthquake (Acts 16:25,26). In a sense, the singing was more of a wonder than the earthquake. Imagine the scene: two men—beaten and bloody, down in the miserable inner prison, uncomfortable in the stocks. What would you have done in that situation? Complain? Exclaim, "How do you like that? What a bad

48

turn of events! Maybe we made a mistake in coming here!"?

At midnight, Paul and Silas were praying and singing. Why? God was with them. Rulers and prisons could not separate them from their Lord. Furthermore, a slave girl had been freed and Lydia had believed. They certainly had great reason for praise.

Other prisoners were listening (v. 25). Remember, we speak most effectively and fruitfully when we praise God in the midst of suffering. People who otherwise would be uninterested in Christ begin to listen.

Paul and Silas are not an isolated case. Down through the centuries God has given His people "songs in the night." Madame Guyon spent ten years of her life in French prisons (1695-1705). Here is a song she wrote in prison, quoted by G. Campbell Morgan in *The Acts of the Apostles,* p. 390:

> A little bird am I
>   Shut from the fields of air;
> And in my cage I sit and sing
>   To Him Who placed me there;
> Well pleased a prisoner to be
> Because, my God, it pleaseth Thee.
>
> Nought have I else to do;
>   I sing the whole day long;
> And He Whom most I love to please,
>   Doth listen to my song;
> He caught and bound my wandering wing,
> But still He bends to hear me sing.

Thou hast an ear to hear;
   A heart to love and bless;
And, though my notes were e'er so rude,
   Thou wouldst not hear the less;
Because Thou knowest, as they fall,
That same, sweet Love, inspires them all.

My cage confines me round;
   Abroad I cannot fly;
But though my wing is closely bound,
   My heart's at liberty.
My prison walls cannot control
The flight, the freedom of the soul.

Oh, it is good to soar
   These bolts and bars above,
To Him Whose purpose I adore,
   Whose providence I love;
And in Thy mighty will to find
The joy, the freedom of the mind.

As Paul and Silas were singing, they felt an earthquake. The foundations of the prison were shaken. The doors fell open. The chains fell off the prisoners. This must have included the stocks into which Paul and Silas had been placed.

The jailer thought all the prisoners had escaped. He was ready to commit suicide, for he would be held responsible for any escape. But Paul assured him that all the prisoners had remained in place. Have you ever wondered why the prisoners didn't flee? I think they realized something tremendous was happening, and they didn't want to miss it.

These events precipitated a great question and answer. The question was "What must I do to be saved?" (v. 30). I'm not sure the jailer understood all the implications of his question. He had never before heard prisoners singing. He experienced the earthquake. He knew that the prisoners had not escaped. He realized he had come to an important moment in his life. These men—Paul and Silas—had what he didn't. So he asked the most important question any person can ask.

Paul could give him the answer in one sentence: "Believe on the Lord Jesus Christ" (v. 31). That's a tribute to the simplicity of the Gospel. But Paul and Silas didn't stop there. They shared God's Word with him and his family (v. 32).

The truth of God's Word produced some wonderful results. The jailer and his entire family believed and were baptized. The prisoners had shown the free man (who was really the prisoner) how he could become free. Do you think some of the other prisoners were saved too? I think so.

As soon as the jailer had heard God's Word, he ministered to Paul and Silas by washing their wounds (v. 33). This must have taken a lot of work. Next, he brought them into his home and put a good meal before them. He acted like Lydia. His open heart resulted in an open home.

The jailer also rejoiced. It always happens that way. When Christ comes in and frees us from sin, the result is joy. When we serve as Jesus' witnesses, we bring joy to others.

The next day, the authorities sent word to the prison that Paul and Silas could go. But Paul said, in essence, "Not on your life. They beat us and threw us into prison without a trial. We are Roman citizens. Let

51

them come and take us out" (v. 37). So the magistrates had to come and eat humble pie.

Why did Paul do this? First, to show that those who have the responsibilities of citizenship also have the privileges of citizenship. Second, to make things easier for the believers in Philippi. It would help others understand that Christianity was not some foolish movement but was embraced by intelligent people who were Roman citizens.

The great lesson of this chapter is *God leads and God works*. We just need to follow.

Chapter 5

The Second Journey:
Evangelizing in Macedonia and Achaia
(Acts 17:1—18:22)

In Acts 17:6 we find an intriguing phrase: "These who have turned the world upside down." This reveals the impact that the Gospel and the missionary team were making wherever they went. By turning the world upside down, they were bringing it right side up because it was upside down in the first place.

On one occasion a little girl was talking about the books of the Bible. She said that the Bible ended with the Book of Revolutions. (Of course, she meant Revelation.) However, she spoke more wisely than she knew. We find plenty of revolution in the New Testament—Gospel revolution. Let's look at how this happened as the second missionary journey continued.

In Thessalonica

Thessalonica lay about 100 miles southwest of Philippi. It had the distinction of being the most populous city in Macedonia. It was the most important center that Paul and his group had visited up to this point. G. Campbell Morgan commented that Thessalonica stood on the highway, while Berea was located on the byway (*The Acts of the Apostles*, p. 398).

The question arises—Why did Paul go *through* Amphipolis and Apollonia and not stop in those places to preach the Gospel? First, he felt that if he planted the Gospel in the strategic center of Thessalonica, the new believers would take the message to Amphipolis and Apollonia. Second, Paul was still following God's direction, and that led to Thessalonica.

Witness

Paul followed the same practice in Thessalonica as he had in previous cities. He went first to the synagogue to witness to the Jews and also to the Greeks. He did this even though the Jews had consistently treated him very shabbily. But he continued to love them. Consequently, he has given us all an example of perseverance in God's work.

Paul continued to give the same basic message (Acts 17:2,3). He told his hearers about the suffering, death and resurrection of Jesus. He explained that this Jesus was the Christ, the anointed of God. In all of his preaching Paul backed up his message from the Scriptures. Even today we know of no better way to share God's message.

Results

Consistently good results come from faithfully preaching God's Word. This was true in Thessalonica: "And some of them were persuaded; and a great multitude of the devout Greeks, and not a few of the

54

leading women, joined Paul and Silas" (Acts 17:4). It is interesting to note that many women were drawn to Christ. They could certainly benefit from the Gospel. Wherever the Gospel has been preached, it has raised the status of women.

This was a tremendous response. When we read I and II Thessalonians, we can see how far the Gospel spread from these believers in Thessalonica. First Thessalonians 1:8 says, "From you the word of the Lord has sounded forth, not only in Macedonia and Achaia, but also in every place."

Riot and Revolution

The unbelieving Jews very quickly began to organize opposition. They mobilized "evil men from the marketplace" (Acts 17:5). We could call them "loafers of the marketplace." They constituted the rabble of Thessalonica. The jealously zealous Jews stopped at nothing in their desire to combat the missionaries.

They set the whole city in an uproar. They even attacked the home of Jason because he had extended hospitality to the missionaries. These Jewish enemies accused the Christian workers of turning the world upside down. They claimed that the Gospel messengers were setting up another king besides Caesar.

In a sense the Jewish zealots were mistaken. Paul and his people were not unpatriotic. They had no plans to overthrow the government or to unseat Caesar. They *were* promoting a kingdom, but it was not of this world.

In another sense Paul's enemies were speaking the

55

truth. The Gospel these people feared was revolutionary. Its message demanded changes in society and in personal life-style. When people believe and obey the Gospel, many things get turned upside down (which really brings them right side up). The angry Jews paid a great compliment to the Christian emissaries when they accused them of turning the world upside down.

The Gospel message is disturbing. God's truth accomplishes what it should—it upsets our sinfulness, our complacency and our selfishness. It disturbs all of us—whether we live in a primitive or a sophisticated society or somewhere in between. Many of us Christians deserve blame for not causing greater upheaval in our society through holy living. Instead of being revolutionaries for God, many of us become quiet bystanders in the midst of a crooked and perverse generation.

Jason and some other believers suffered most from the angry mob. They were dragged before the rulers, which didn't happen gently. No doubt the Gospel haters became more incensed when they realized that Paul and Silas had disappeared.

Jason and his supporters had to post a significant bond before the authorities would release them. This may have included the promise of not permitting Paul and his company to return, at least for a stated period. But the missionaries had sown the Gospel seed, and God was giving the increase. The believers in Thessalonica would stand as a great example of faith, love and patience (see I Thess. 1). From them, the Word of the Lord went forth, not only in Macedonia and Achaia but in every place.

In Berea

Faithful believers had whisked Paul and Silas out of Thessalonica (Acts 17:10). They arranged for them to go by night to Berea, about 60 miles to the west. At that point, some of us might have said, "Things are getting pretty grim. Maybe we should quit while we're still ahead."

However, look at Paul and Silas. As soon as they arrived in Berea, they preached the Gospel. Furthermore, they went again to the local synagogue, even though they had encountered much opposition in synagogues in other cities. What a spirit of dedication to the Lord's mission! When David Livingstone was once asked where he was prepared to go, he replied with that same spirit, "I am prepared to go anywhere, *so long as it is forward*" (quoted in *The Acts of the Apostles*, by William Barclay, p. 129).

Noble Attitude

The Berean Jews and Greeks exhibited a different attitude from that of the Thessalonian Jews. They listened to the message with open-minded attention. They didn't allow prejudice to block their thinking. But they did insist that the preaching of the visitors be tested by the Scriptures. They held to this principle so firmly that they searched the Scriptures daily.

The Bible says they had noble character (Acts 17:11, KJV). We need to have these same qualities — being open minded and ready to listen but always subjecting what we hear to the test of God's Word.

It's no wonder that many churches and societies

have chosen the name Berean. If they remain true to that name, they will serve fruitfully for God's glory.

Good Fruit

Many of the Jews believed and also a good number of Greeks (Acts 17:12). Prominent men and women were included in both groups. Any Christian worker would rejoice to see that kind of response.

The abundant result would lead us to conclude that the Berean congregation would figure very prominently in the life of the early church. Maybe it did. But it does surprise us that we do not hear any more about the Berean fellowship—either in The Acts of the Apostles or in the epistles. Prominence, however, does not determine importance or lack of it. Since we do not have any contrary evidence, I assume that these noble people of Berea continued faithfully in the Lord's work. The Holy Spirit must have had His own special reason for not mentioning them again, just as He did in leaving Philip the evangelist out of the record after his early appearances.

Continuing Opposition

Once more the determined adversaries did their best to disrupt the work of the Lord. Just as on other occasions, Jews came from another city to stir up trouble (Acts 17:13). The crowd became aroused even in this city of fair-minded people.

So again it became necessary for Paul to leave the city, although Silas and Timothy were able to remain. Loyal Christian friends took Paul to Athens, about 100 miles to the southeast. In Acts we see a continuing story of *trial* and *triumph.* The same holds true today. Remember Acts 14:22. The apostles spoke truly when they advised the new believers: "We must through many tribulations enter the kingdom of God."

In Athens

Paul waited in Athens for Silas and Timothy. Much more happened while he was waiting than Paul or the others anticipated.

Paul's Agony

It's very instructive to see what a man like Paul will do while waiting. As W. Graham Scroggie said, "Paul did more while he waited than some folk do when they are working" (*The Acts of the Apostles,* p. 129).

Paul became indignant, provoked and burdened when he saw the idolatry of Athens (Acts 17:16). Most people who visited Athens would spend their time observing the greatness of its art, architecture and culture. But Paul saw the desperate need of perishing human beings.

I wonder how we look at the great cities of our day. Expositor G. Campbell Morgan said, "Our cities are as full of idols as was Athens" (*The Acts of the Apostles,* p. 415).

Athenian Flippancy

When some Epicureans and Stoics encountered Paul, they called him a babbler (Acts 17:18). That word can also be translated "seed picker," giving us the picture of a hungry bird who is fluttering around looking for food. However, these philosophers exhibited

59

curiosity about his new doctrine. After all, the Athenians wanted only "to tell or to hear some new thing" (v. 21).

Athens had lost a great deal of its former glory. True, it was still a famous city and a great cultural center. But even its most laudable philosophies had degenerated. The Stoics at one time exalted virtue. Now they had become immoral fatalists whose highest virtue was suicide. The Epicureans formerly advocated a good kind of pleasure. Now they had descended to the most sinful lust.

Among these quick-witted and flippant folks, Paul gave his witness. He did this in three places—in the synagogue among the Jews and Greeks, in the marketplace with anyone who was present and, finally, at the Areopagus. The Areopagus was the Supreme Court of Athens. It was a court of about 30 judges who ruled on cases of homicide and public morals. Apparently, they also liked to listen to new philosophies. To this impressive group, the philosophers conducted Paul. What a responsibility and privilege!

Appropriate Message

Paul certainly knew how to adapt his message to every audience. He began by starting on common ground with the Athenians. He didn't insult them. He noted they were very religious (Acts 17:22). He mentioned an important matter they immediately understood. Among the many altars in Athens, at least one bore the inscription: "To the unknown god." Then Paul said, "I'll tell you about that God" (see v. 23).

Notice the important themes Paul covered. First,

60

God is the Creator (vv. 24,25). Second, He has guided history (v. 26). Third, He has done this so that all men will seek Him (v. 27). Fourth, the day of groping and ignorance is past (v. 30). Fifth, the Day of Judgment is coming (v. 31). Sixth, the fact that Christ rose from the dead proves He is the Judge (v. 31). *Amidst the great philosophers of that day, this man of God called them all to repentance.*

Mixed Response

The response in Athens was typical of what we often see when the Gospel is preached. Some mocked. Others procrastinated. Some believed. Or stating it another way—some caused *division,* others *delayed,* while some made the right *decision.*

We can thank the Lord that even in spiritually bankrupt Athens, Paul saw fruit. One of the new believers, Dionysius, was a member of the Areopagus. A woman, Damaris, also believed. She probably represented a sector of society that was not very respectable, because respectable women wouldn't have been there in public. In addition to these specifically named, others also believed.

We don't hear any more about Athens in Acts. However, we do know from other historical records that some good Christian leaders came from this center of bankrupt human philosophy.

In Corinth

Corinth was a great commercial center but also a corrupt center. Writers have described its character as "abysmal profligacy and abundant immorality."

Corinth had become a byword for corruption. The temple to Aphrodite was located here. In the temple, 1000 priestesses were nothing more than prostitutes. Paul wrote Romans 1 while he was in Corinth. When Paul later wrote to the Corinthians, he described what kind of sinners some of them had been (I Cor. 6:9-11). He spent more than 18 months in Corinth.

Paul met Priscilla and Aquila in Corinth (Acts 18:2). They had recently come from Rome. Claudius had ordered the Jews to leave that city. Priscilla and Aquila were tentmakers, as Paul was. So the three of them began to work together. This contact resulted in a long and positive association in the Lord's work (see Rom. 16:3; I Cor. 16:19; II Tim. 4:19).

We know from other passages that Paul often worked at his trade (see I Cor. 4:11,12; I Thess. 2:9). Rabbis regularly learned a trade, since it was not considered proper for them to charge for services. Paul, as a former rabbi, followed the same custom. In Tarsus, Paul's hometown, they made a cloth from goat's hair that they used for tentmaking. They called this cloth "cilicium," because it came from the province of Cilicia.

When Timothy and Silas came to Corinth, they probably brought funds as well as encouraging reports from Macedonia (see Phil. 4:15,16; I Thess. 3:6). Therefore, Paul could work less in tentmaking and give more time to Gospel outreach.

Rejected by the Jews

Once more Paul began his work in the synagogue, preaching to both Jews and Greeks (Acts 18:4). Again the Jews opposed him. Then he said, "Your blood be upon your own heads; I am clean. From now on I will go to the Gentiles" (v. 6).

Accepted by Justus, Crispus and Others

Though it hurt Paul to be rejected by his own people, he also received much encouragement in Corinth by seeing the great fruit God gave. Justus, who lived next door to the synagogue, believed. Then Crispus, the very ruler of the synagogue, believed—along with all his household. But that wasn't all. Many other Corinthians, after hearing what had happened, believed and were baptized. What a change that must have been for many of them!

Encouraged by the Lord

God then spoke to Paul at night by a vision (Acts 18:9,10). He knew that Paul needed encouragement, so God gave him a great promise and a directive:
1. Do not fear.
2. Speak and do not keep silent.
3. I am with you and will protect you.
4. I have many people in this city.

No wonder Paul found it possible to continue and to do it with enthusiasm! I love that phrase "many people in this city" (v. 10). God promises the same today. Take heart!

Helped by Gallio

Gallio was the brother of the Roman philosopher Seneca. He was noted for his kindness. While Paul was in Corinth, Gallio became proconsul of Achaia. This seemed to prompt the Jews to unite in an attack on

Paul. They brought him to the judgment seat (Acts 18:12). Gallio made it plain he did not think Paul was doing anything worthy of judgment. He declared that Paul's religious activity was permitted under the laws of Rome.

Then the whole matter reversed. The Greeks rose up this time. They seized the ruler of the synagogue, Sosthenes, and beat him in front of the judgment seat. Gallio did nothing. He no doubt thought that Sosthenes deserved it, because he had incited the insurrection.

In Concluding the Journey

Paul was now ready to leave Corinth. He sailed for Syria (Acts 18:18). In Cenchrea, the eastern port of Corinth, he had his hair cut off. This probably indicated the end of a Nazarite vow he had taken (see Num. 6:1-21). He had no doubt taken this vow during his missionary work in Corinth. It might have been after he was constrained by the Spirit (Acts 18:5) or after the Lord had given him a great promise (vv. 9,10). Was he right or wrong for doing this? We can't know for sure.

Paul stopped only briefly in Ephesus, because he planned to return later for a longer time (vv. 19-21). He did go to Jerusalem, probably to attend the Passover Feast. Then he returned to Antioch. What a trip this second missionary journey had been! No doubt he rehearsed all that God had done and how He had opened the door to many hearts.

Chapter 6

The Third Journey:
God's Word Growing Mightily in Ephesus
(Acts 18:23—19:41)

It's beautiful to see Paul's concern both for new Christians and for the unevangelized. He could have remained permanently in Antioch. However, after a time, he started out again (Acts 18:23). First, he went through all of Galatia and Phrygia, strengthening all the disciples. Next, he returned to Ephesus as he had promised. One of his greatest challenges awaited him there.

The Powerful Preaching of Apollos

Apollos came from Alexandria in Egypt. That city was renowned as a center of Greek culture. About one million Jews lived in Alexandria. Like Paul, Apollos had been exposed to two cultures. He had received good Old Testament training, and he had been educated in Greek culture.

His Ability in the Scriptures

Apollos possessed great natural gifts in combination with knowledge and effectiveness in the Scriptures. Acts 18:24 describes him as an "eloquent man." The

Greek word translated "eloquent" includes the idea of oratorical ability as well as extensive knowledge. In other words, he was a learned man with the gift of articulating and applying his knowledge.

Along with his special gifts, Apollos was "fervent in spirit" (v. 25). The Greek word literally means "boiling in spirit." This same word appears in Romans 12:11, where we are urged to be "not lagging in diligence, fervent in spirit, serving the Lord." Though possessing much knowledge, Apollos didn't have a bloated head. He had a burning heart.

But this unusual man lacked some important knowledge and experience. "He knew only the baptism of John" (v. 25). John the Baptist had preached repentance and the coming of the Messiah. Apollos had learned that lesson well. But he had not heard the message of grace, liberty and power in Jesus Christ. No doubt he knew the facts of the life, ministry, death and resurrection of the Lord Jesus. Yet he had not been able to fit it into God's plan of salvation offered to all men.

His Acceptance of Instruction

Priscilla and Aquila came to the rescue. "They took him aside and explained to him the way of God more accurately" (Acts 18:26). We see two marvelous lessons here. First, Priscilla and Aquila helped Apollos instead of criticizing him. Such a mighty man could have intimidated them or made them jealous. But they recognized his potential and realized he could not do a lasting work unless he learned the missing truths. So they enthusiastically provided the assistance he needed.

Second, Apollos accepted their teaching with a positive spirit. Being as gifted as he was, he could have rejected their aid. Instead, his heart was open to learn all he could. We can profit from his example. Unfortunately, some of us say by our actions, "Don't confuse me with the facts. My mind is made up."

With a more complete understanding of the Gospel, Apollos entered an even more effective ministry. He received letters of recommendation from his colleagues in Ephesus and went over to Corinth. There "he greatly helped those who had believed through grace; for he vigorously refuted the Jews publicly, showing from the Scriptures that Jesus is the Christ" (vv. 27,28). Paul later made a very complimentary reference to the ministry of Apollos when he said: "I planted, Apollos watered, but God gave the increase" (I Cor. 3:6).

Thomas Walker in *Acts of the Apostles* (page 436) summarizes the characteristics of Apollos as presented in verses 24-28:

(a) Facility in speaking—verse 24.
(b) Efficiency in Bible knowledge—verse 24.
(c) Sincerity in testimony—verse 25. (Teaching clearly all he actually knew.)
(d) Fervency of spirit—verse 25.
(e) Docility of disposition—verse 26. (Ready to learn.)
(f) Constancy in labour—verse 27. (Ready for new efforts.)
(g) Ability in service—verses 27,28. (Helping the Christians. Evangelizing the non-Christians.)

The Helping Hand for New Disciples

After Apollos had left for Corinth, Paul arrived in Ephesus. He soon encountered a handful of disciples whose knowledge and experience were similar to that of Apollos.

Their Experience With John's Baptism

Paul must have noticed quickly that something was lacking in their understanding of the Gospel. So he asked them, "Did you receive the Holy Spirit when you believed?" (Acts 19:2). They replied, "We have not so much as heard whether there is a Holy Spirit" (v. 2). We don't know all they meant by that answer. If they had studied the Old Testament, they would have been familiar with references to the Spirit of the Lord. They apparently knew nothing, however, about the ministry of the Holy Spirit in the life of a believer.

Like Apollos, these believers knew much about John's baptism, which emphasized repentance and preparing for the coming of Messiah. They did not understand the baptism of Jesus, which symbolized forgiveness of sins and salvation by grace through faith.

Their Entrance Into Holy Spirit Baptism

Paul explained clearly that John had prepared the way for the Lord Jesus. Having repented, they should trust the Redeemer to bring them into the glorious liberty of the sons of God (Acts 19:4). These immature believers must have rejoiced in that good news.

Then Paul arranged for them to be baptized in the

name of Jesus. When Paul laid hands on them, the Holy Spirit came upon them as described in I Corinthians 12:13. They were baptized into the Body of Christ. At the same time, they received special spiritual gifts, which they manifested by speaking in tongues and prophesying. This is the last time speaking in tongues is mentioned in Acts.

Why did the Holy Spirit choose to include this unusual account in Acts? Two reasons come to mind. First, to reemphasize that every true believer has the indwelling Holy Spirit to lead him to maturity in the Christian life. The Holy Spirit belongs to those who trust Christ, and they should belong to Him completely. Second, to signal (through the granting of special gifts) that another decisive moment had arrived in missionary history. Ephesus was becoming a new center of Gentile mission. God was preparing these new believers, along with the Apostle Paul, for a great ministry among Gentiles.

The Mighty Ministry of Paul

The Gospel movement began to gain momentum in Ephesus. Before examining the actual events, let's learn more about Ephesus. It was the marketplace of Asia Minor. It had the honor of being an Assize town. This means that a Roman governor visited Ephesus regularly for the purpose of trying cases.

Besides these distinctions, Ephesus was famous as the center of Diana worship. The temple to Diana was 425 feet long, 225 feet wide and 60 feet high and was supported by 127 pillars. The image of Diana (Latin-Diana, Greek-Artemis) was quite ugly. This many-

69

breasted figure—black and squat—symbolized fertility. Some think that the image was actually a meteorite that had fallen to earth. The temple had become an asylum for criminals. Furthermore, it served as a banking center for the busy commerce of Ephesus.

The city of Ephesus stood as the very center of pagan superstition. The people believed in charms and magic. They used documents and parchments that they called "Ephesian letters." The populace believed with a passion that these letters would protect them from danger, give good success in their business affairs and help them in numerous other ways.

In the Synagogue

Paul plunged into the work at Ephesus just as he had in many other places. He went into the synagogue and "spoke boldly for three months, reasoning and persuading concerning the things of the kingdom of God" (Acts 19:8). The more he testified, the more some hearers became hardened in their unbelief. They began to speak evil of Christianity to many others. They were actively mobilizing to oppose Paul.

The apostle took drastic action. At times we must do the same. He disassociated himself from the synagogue and the people there. He took with him those who had become followers of the Lord Jesus. In other words, he left the "fellowship" of the synagogue and started a new congregation. He certainly had good reason for taking this step. He didn't make this separation until the situation became impossible. Often, through the years, God's people have faced comparable alternatives—to stay or to go. We should never break fellowship for frivolous or unworthy reasons. On the other hand, we should have the courage to separate when the people among whom we serve oppose God's purpose and resist His true message.

In the School of Tyrannus

Opposition didn't daunt Paul, as we have already learned from other experiences. The closing door of the synagogue enabled Paul to find the open door in the school of Tyrannus (Acts 19:9). Paul probably couldn't help but remember that he, too, had fought fiercely against the Way, just as some of his compatriots were doing now (see 9:1,2).

Tyrannus must have been a well-known philosopher and teacher. We can conclude that Paul used these facilities at a time when Tyrannus was not conducting his classes. Paul must have gathered his people during the middle of the day, which was "siesta" time in Ephesus.

An interesting picture emerges. Paul probably worked at his trade in the morning and late afternoon. In the middle of the day, when many Ephesians were resting, Paul was reasoning in the school of Tyrannus. Paul told the Ephesian elders in Acts 20:34, "Yes, you yourselves know that these hands have provided for my necessities, and for those who were with me." Paul carried on this demanding schedule for two years— making tents, preaching and teaching in the school of Tyrannus, and providing pastoral care for the believers.

God blessed this earnest effort. "All who dwelt in Asia heard the word of the Lord Jesus, both Jews and Greeks" (19:10). That happened in two ways. First, many hearers must have attended the lectures in the school of Tyrannus. People came to Ephesus from many places because the city was a great crossroads. So Paul had a varied and changing audience. Second, the nonresidents who heard Paul eventually returned to their home areas. Some of them received the Lord Jesus through Paul's witness. They carried the Good News with them wherever they went.

In Signs and Wonders

The Lord didn't use Paul only as a verbal witness. He worked unusual miracles through him (Acts 19:11). We can understand why God chose to work that way. The Ephesians trusted in their charms, magic and letters. Down deep many of them must have realized that much of what they believed in was phony. Now God was displaying the genuine article through Paul. This must have astounded the Ephesians.

God worked very dramatically through Paul. People even carried his work clothes to the sick and the possessed, and they were healed (v. 12). The handkerchiefs were really the sweatbands Paul used on his head while he was working. The aprons, of course, were worn while he stood at his workbench.

What should we conclude from this story? That God wants us to do this with the clothes of prominent preachers and teachers? Not at all. When God worked that way in Ephesus, He did not set a pattern for generations to follow. What we can learn is that the God whom we serve has adequate power to meet the needs of His work wherever it is carried on. He displays that strength in a variety of ways for every situation. I can testify joyfully, after 40 years of missionary service, that God still works mightily today. He especially does this by changing lives through His Word energized by His Spirit.

The Complete Consecration of Many Believers

When great things happen by God's power, many people like to get into the act without submitting their lives to God's rule. When some Jewish exorcists saw what God was accomplishing through Paul, they also tried to use the power (Acts 19:13). They attempted to cast out evil spirits in the name of Jesus.

Preceded by the Humiliation of Sceva's Sons

Acts 19:14 refers to seven sons of a man named Sceva, a Jewish chief priest. We do not know if Sceva held the title of chief priest legitimately or if he took that title by himself. At any rate, his sons tried to use the name of Jesus to cast out evil spirits. But the attempt backfired. The evil spirit said, "Jesus I know, and Paul I know; but who are you?" (v. 15). Then the spirit-possessed man attacked them violently, leaving them wounded and naked. The incident should stand as a solemn warning to all who seek to manipulate the power of God without truly belonging to the God of power. Furthermore, when we belong to the God of power, we will take great care to give God the glory— as Paul did. We will not take the credit ourselves.

Proven by the Burning of Their Charms

People throughout the city—both Jews and Greeks—heard about what had happened to Sceva's sons (Acts 19:17). The news filled the citizens of Ephesus, including the believers, with fear. Those who had been living indifferently now began to magnify the name of the Lord Jesus.

Believers came forward to confess their sins and reveal the secrets behind their magic spells (v. 18). We can conclude from these statements that some believers had not yet left their old practices of charms and magic. They had trusted the Lord, but they continued to cling to their old letters and amulets. Now many of these believers came to the place of total surrender. They ceased trusting the old magic and believed only in their Almighty Lord.

Today, in this age, we would do well to give ourselves to the Lord as those people did. We have many practices in our Christian churches that dishonor God and limit His power in our lives. A time of confession where we lay aside the sin that so easily ensnares us (Heb. 12:1) and reconsecrate our lives to the Lord of lords would be appropriate action and would result in spiritual benefit.

In addition to their verbal confession, the believers proved their sincerity by publicly burning their charms and letters (Acts 19:19). These books were not the same as books today. They were parchments and letters with magic charms and spells written on them. They did this in full view of the city; it was not done secretly. In Ephesus, where people depended so greatly upon magic and charms, this must have made a great impression. These articles also had a price attached to them. Estimates vary concerning how much 50,000 pieces of silver would be worth today. But the narrative definitely gives the impression that a great deal of material value went up in smoke. These Ephesian believers willingly made this sacrifice. Like Moses, they esteemed "the reproach of Christ greater riches than the treasures in Egypt" (Heb. 11:26).

So the Word of the Lord "grew mightily and prevailed" (Acts 19:20). Three important factors contributed to the success of the Gospel ministry in Ephesus. First, the leader (Paul) gave his witness with full dedication. Second, God worked special signs and miracles. Third, a purified church contributed to the effective outreach.

At this point, Paul sensed that the Spirit was compelling him to go through Macedonia and Achaia, then to Jerusalem and finally to Rome (v. 21). Yet he also understood the need for continuing the good work in Ephesus. He met the call by sending Timothy and Erastus to Macedonia, while he remained in Ephesus. Many think Paul desired to go to Jerusalem to deliver the offering that had been collected for the saints there (see I Cor. 16:1-4).

It is probable that Paul wrote I Corinthians during his time at Ephesus. Of his ministry at that time, Paul testified, "For a great and effective door has opened to me, and there are many adversaries" (v. 9).

The Unbridled Uproar in the City

The Gospel was advancing so powerfully in Ephesus that it began to threaten some of the business interests in the city. Many artisans made a prosperous living by producing little shrines of Diana.

Instigated by Demetrius

Demetrius, a silversmith, held a position of leadership among the craftsmen of the city. He brought the workers together and warned them about the inroads the Gospel message was making. His language lets us realize how powerfully the Gospel was advancing. He said, "You see and hear that not only at Ephesus, but throughout almost all Asia, this Paul has persuaded and turned away many people, saying that they are not gods which are made with hands" (Acts 19:26).

Demetrius not only appealed to their financial interests but also to their religious devotion. He persuaded his colleagues that Diana could lose her temple and her magnificence unless they could stop the Gospel advance.

Intensified by Many

The crowd responded with passion and fury. They all began to yell, "Great is Diana of the Ephesians!" (Acts 19:28). The more they cried out, the more confused the citizens became. Have you ever witnessed a mob in action—or gotten caught in a riot? I have had this experience on several occasions in missionary service. I especially remember one time. The crowd was parading on the run through a principal street. From all sides, folks came running to join the group. As one man rushed by, I asked him what it was all about. He answered in Spanish, "No se, pero que viva" (I don't know, but may he live).

The crowd in Ephesus rushed into the theater, which could accommodate about 25,000 people. They seized two of Paul's companions, Gaius and Aristarchus, and dragged them in with them. When Paul learned what had happened, he wanted to join the crowd and speak to the rioters. But his fellow disciples prevented him. Even some top Asian officials pleaded with him not to venture into the theater. That shows that Paul had a good reputation among certain officials. They realized that this servant of Christ was living lawfully as a good citizen. Perhaps some of them believed secretly.

Another drama occurred. In the theater, the Jews pushed a man named Alexander forward as their spokesman. They obviously wanted Alexander to disassociate the Jewish population from the ministry of Paul and those who believed with him. However, that stratagem didn't work. When they realized Alexander was a Jew, the crowd was stirred even more. They cried out for two hours, "Great is Diana of the Ephesians!" (v. 34). What a scene that must have been.

Interrupted by the Town Clerk

The town clerk was an important official. He feared that the riot would get out of hand. If that occurred, Rome would hold him responsible. The clerk spoke very wisely. First, he told the crowd that Diana's greatness could not be denied (Acts 19:35,36). Then, he affirmed that Paul and his companions were not lawbreakers (v. 37). However, if the rioters felt they had a genuine case against Paul, they could take it to the courts (v. 38). Finally, the clerk reminded them that if they continued to riot, they would be in danger of breaking Roman law (vv. 39,40). He succeeded in quieting and dismissing the crowd.

Contemplating this scene, we understand why Paul later wrote to the Ephesians: "We do not wrestle against flesh and blood, but against principalities, against powers, against the rulers of the darkness of this age, against spiritual hosts of wickedness in the heavenly places. Therefore take up the whole armor of God" (Eph. 6:12,13).

Chapter 7

The Third Journey: Continuing the Course
(Acts 20:1-38)

Acts 20 provides an excellent look at Paul, the missionary, in action. His ministry in Ephesus had ended with a city-wide uproar. But, more importantly, the Gospel had transformed many people in that important city. "The word of the Lord grew mightily and prevailed" (Acts 19:20).

Instant in Season and out of Season

Did Paul say at this point, "That's enough. I've done my share. The battle is becoming too tough"? No, he knew how to be "instant in season, out of season" (II Tim. 4:2, KJV). He knew that he hadn't yet finished the course God had planned for him. He knew he must still encourage the new believers and take the Gospel to new places and peoples.

Encouraging Ministry in Macedonia and Achaia

The Gospel had really taken root in Macedonia. The cities of Philippi, Thessalonica and Berea all had flourishing congregations. Paul journeyed there again, not as a tourist but as an inspirer. He "encouraged them

79

with many words" (Acts 20:2). We see Paul, the pastor, giving his very best energy and experience to help his fellow believers in the Christian life. Encouragement is a great ministry. Often we fail to realize its importance.

Besides helping the converts in Macedonia, Paul exercised a writing ministry to other areas. During this period he probably penned II Corinthians. We can all thank God that he invested the time to give the Corinthian church and succeeding generations that valuable epistle.

From Macedonia Paul advanced to Greece (Achaia). It's possible that, before he went south, he made a special point of evangelizing Illyricum. He referred to that region in Romans 15:19. In Greece he no doubt gave most of the time to Corinth and Athens. He remained for three months in that area.

It appears that Paul wrote Romans during his stay in Corinth. He sent the epistle with Phoebe, a deaconess of the church at Cenchrea (Rom. 16:1). The time period probably included the winter months of A.D. 56-57.

Evading the Enemy Once More

Paul had planned to go from Greece directly to Syria and on to Jerusalem in time for Passover. However, his determined enemies continued to harass him. Paul found out that the Jews were hatching a plot against him (Acts 20:3). They no doubt thought they could arrange to have him thrown overboard on the trip from Greece to Syria.

Once more Paul had to change plans. He decided to

return through Macedonia. He probably did this by land, at least for the first part of the journey. A good group of friends accompanied him (v. 4). At some point, these colleagues went on ahead to Troas. Luke now rejoined Paul, having been absent for a long time. This is indicated by the use of the word "us" in verse 5. The most plausible conclusion is that Luke had been serving the church in Philippi during his absence. When Paul returned to that city, it was time for Luke to join the apostle again. Paul and Luke spent the time of the Passover in Philippi. Then, after a five-day trip by sea from Philippi, they rejoined the group at Troas.

Insight Into Paul's Priorities

Paul and his group stayed for seven days in Troas (Acts 20:6). At first glance the story of what happened there seems strange.

A Fervent Fellowship

When the disciples in Troas came together, Paul preached to them. As the story unfolds, we are inclined to think we are looking at a long-winded preacher (Paul) and a short-winded listener (Eutychus). The Bible tells us that, as Paul continued speaking, Eutychus sank into a deep sleep (Acts 20:9). No doubt, the third-story room was filled with people. We have the picture of a large congregation. The room apparently lacked sufficient ventilation. The burning of many candles or lamps would have used some of the available oxygen, compounding the problem. Possibly Eutychus had worked hard that day. When we combine all these factors, we can understand why sleep overcame him.

Eutychus lost his balance and fell out of the third-floor window to the ground. They all thought he was dead. Paul immediately went down to where the young man lay. He fell on the young man, embraced him and said, "Do not trouble yourselves, for his life is in him" (v. 10). Paul's actions remind us of what Elijah and Elisha did in similar situations (I Kings 17:21; II Kings 4:34). The young man then recovered (Acts 20:12).

What was the significance of this whole event? We are really looking at a Sunday worship service made more important by Paul's presence. The possibility existed that he was gathering with them for the last time.

The believers had come together to "break bread" (v. 7). In the early church the Christians regularly had a fellowship meal followed by the observance of the Lord's Supper. The meal often was the best of the week for some of the believers, particularly the slaves who attended the services.

Paul was leading the group in worship. The word translated "spoke" really means "discoursed." In other words, although Paul served as the leader, he didn't do all the talking. The believers shared in the conversation and fellowship. The meeting continued for a number of hours. It's wonderful to see how people can forget time when they are gathered in the presence of the living Lord.

Paul was much more than a long-winded preacher. We observe him in this scene as a burdened, intense, devoted man. Even after the fall of Eutychus, Paul continued to encourage and teach the believers. The gathering didn't end until daybreak. When the service ended, they brought Eutychus in to show that he was indeed alive. This brought great comfort to everyone present.

What lessons can we learn from this incident? Do we have the same lively interest in eternal matters that Paul and these people did? Unfortunately, we often give more time to temporal things than we do to eternal concerns. We happily give hours to some athletic, cultural or entertainment event. Then we come late to a one-hour morning worship service and become impatient when it goes a few minutes beyond noon.

This story of the meeting in Troas challenges us to "take time to be holy." This doesn't happen automatically through long church services or by an endless round of church activities. But it does occur through giving our best time to the right priorities. We become what we read, see, hear and feed on.

One day some people asked a young minister, "Do you have a strong church?" He replied, "Yes." They asked, "How many members do you have?" He said, "30." They exclaimed, "Only 30? Are they wealthy?" "No," he said, "most of them are poor." His questioners then remarked, "How, then, can you call it a strong church?" He calmly replied, "Because they are earnest, devoted, at peace with one another, loving each other, following the Word of God in all things, instant in prayer and striving together to do the Lord's work."

That congregation, as well as the group in Troas, should be an example to us. They were taking time to be holy—and were truly strong as a result.

A Servant's Satisfaction

Paul's companions preceded him by ship to Assos (Acts 20:13). Paul probably remained behind for two reasons. First, some believers in the Troas meeting wished to speak with him afterwards. Second, the walk of about 20 miles by himself to Assos would give him time for meditation and prayer.

Paul joined the missionary group at Assos. Then they traveled by ship to Samos, Trogyllium and Miletus. Paul made the decision not to stop at Ephesus because he could not afford the time this would require. He longed to get to Jerusalem for the Day of Pentecost. However, he did send a message to the elders in Ephesus, asking them to meet him in Miletus (about a 30-mile journey). They responded positively. After they arrived, Paul spoke with them and to them in a beautiful farewell conversation.

The Elements of Such a Life. In his message to the Ephesian elders, Paul expressed satisfaction in knowing that he had done the will of God. It's helpful to examine the specific items he mentioned.

First, he had faithfully declared God's message. He preached the Word both publicly and from house to house. He had warned everyone "night and day with tears" of the consequences of rejecting his message (Acts 20:31). Consequently, he could say that he was innocent of the blood of all men. Second, he had not sought gain for himself. He had worked to pay for his own necessities. Many leaders and followers fall into the trap of loving money and material goods. Each one of us would do well to follow Paul's example (and that of the Lord Jesus) in this regard. He had lived by the principle, "It is more blessed to give than to receive" (v. 35). Third, he had served the Lord with humility of mind. Therefore, he could say, "You know . . . in what manner I always lived among you" (v. 18).

The Expectation of Such a Life. We can see that Paul was looking back with satisfaction at the way he had lived and served. Such contemplation gave him great peace. Furthermore, we know from his other writings that he was looking forward to blessing and reward. In his second letter to Timothy, he affirmed, "Finally, there is laid up for me the crown of righteousness, which the Lord, the righteous Judge, will give to me on that Day, and not to me only but also to all who have loved His appearing" (4:8).

Two classes of people look back on life. First, those who have served God. They are inspired and encouraged by the backward look. Second, those who have veered away from God's course. They look back with regret and sadness.

The Example of Such a Life. Paul's life and conduct sets an example for us. He followed Christ, who ultimately is our example. We, too, should be committed to the will of God. "He who does the will of God abides forever" (I John 2:17). Today we often mistakenly put great emphasis on our standard of living, our comfort and our convenience. However, these do not represent the center and core of life. Serving the Lord and others makes life worthwhile.

A Grand Goal

In Acts 20:24 Paul forcibly expressed his grand goal. I consider this the climax of his testimony to the Ephesian elders and to us.

The Commitment. Essentially, Paul said that only one thing really mattered. He had committed his life to that priority. He targeted his life to finish the course God had given him. Specifically, he dedicated his resources and talents to carrying out the ministry of testifying to the Gospel of the grace of God. Nothing could move him from that course. Everything else had to fall into place around that goal.

It's inspiring to see his clear focus. Paul's life wasn't fragmented, flying in all directions like buckshot. He had aimed it like a rifle bullet to hit the bull's-eye of God's purpose. Without such clear commitment, life can become very fuzzy. It will lack direction. Paul expressed his commitment in another way when he said, "One thing I do, . . . I press toward the goal for the prize of the upward call of God in Christ Jesus" (Phil. 3:13,14).

The Consequences. Because of his strong commitment, Paul could say, "I [do not] count my life dear to myself" (Acts 20:24). In other words, he was so dedicated to doing God's will that he would willingly invest or lose his life for it. For some of us, our primary goal is to preserve and protect our life. But our priority should be to give our life to God for His purposes. He will take care of us.

At the end of the film *Through Gates of Splendor,* Elisabeth Elliot comments on the sacrifice of the five young men who gave their lives in the jungles of Ecuador, South America. They were seeking to reach the Auca Indians with the Gospel. Elisabeth makes the unusual statement: "They succeeded, not in taking the Gospel to the Aucas, but they succeeded in doing what they had set out to do—*they obeyed God."*

The Call. God is calling us to live our lives as Paul did. We should not follow the crowd. We should follow the Lord. Unfortunately, many of us want to be spared the difficulties. We look for a long, peaceful life with a calm sunset. We want everything to go just right. If it doesn't, we think tragedy has struck. We want to save our lives instead of doing God's will. Like one of the five missionaries martyred in Ecuador, we should say, "O God, I'd rather die now than live a life of ease in so sick a world." Another of the five, Jim Elliot, penned these immortal words while he was still a college student: "He is no fool who gives what he cannot keep to gain what he cannot lose." When Henry Martyn arrived in India for missionary service, he declared, "Now let me burn out for God."

I'm told that a number of years ago Phil Hill, then the world's top car-racing driver, was urged by his close friends to abandon racing because of its dangers. He reportedly replied, "Only when I love motor racing less will I value my life more, and only then will I be less willing to risk it." We might question Phil's priority, but we cannot question his commitment. How much more should we say with Paul, "I do not count my life dear to myself"!

87

A Compassionate Concern

Aside from the Lord Jesus, Paul's greatest love was reserved for the church and fellow believers. We saw this in his ministry in Troas. We also see it here in his meeting with the Ephesian elders. In II Corinthians 11:28 he spoke of his "deep concern for all the churches."

Paul demonstrated his love as he spoke with the Ephesian elders. *He warned them* about the dangers without and within the church. They would face "savage wolves" from the outside and saboteurs from the inside (Acts 20:29,30). Such attacks and dangers laid a special responsibility on the elders of Ephesus— and all succeeding elders. Paul urged them to examine their own lives and to be concerned about their flock of believers. More than ever Christian elders need to recognize the greatness of their responsibility and privilege in the service of the Lord and His Church.

He committed them tenderly to God and to His Word (v. 32). Paul's words breathed love. It's obvious that he had a deep affection for his brothers and sisters in Christ. *He prayed with them all.* This prayer time ended very emotionally, with all of them weeping freely. The elders embraced Paul with great love. They were sorrowful because the apostle had told them they would not see him again.

We find important instruction in this part of Paul's time with the elders. We never go wrong when we are deeply concerned about the welfare of the church. Are you and I that kind of church member? Do we make a valuable contribution to our local church—and to believers everywhere? It's good to ask ourselves these questions:

—Am I a knocker or a booster?
—Am I a critic or an encourager?
—Am I a "chief" or a servant?

As we review Acts 20, we should evaluate our priorities. Do we follow the example of Paul and of the Lord Jesus? Jesus said, "My food is to do the will of Him who sent Me, and to finish His work" (John 4:34).

Chapter 8

The Third Journey:
Making Difficult Choices
(Acts 21:1-40)

Amy Carmichael once wrote a poem all of us should read periodically:

> From prayer that asks that I may be
> Sheltered from winds that beat on Thee,
> From fearing when I should aspire,
> From faltering when I should climb higher,
> From silken self, O Captain, free
> Thy soldier who would follow Thee.
>
> From subtle love of softening things,
> From easy choices, weakenings,
> Not thus were spirits fortified,
> Not this way went the Crucified.
> From all that dims Thy Calvary,
> O Lamb of God, deliver me.
>
> (*Toward Jerusalem*, p. 94).

The Apostle Paul stood ready to make difficult choices in doing the will of God. Remember his commitment, expressed in Acts 20:24. He was ready to suffer or even die if that was God's will for him as he continued his ministry. We should have that same type of commitment.

Difficult Choice of Suffering

Before we look at the serious question Paul faced, we need to follow his travels on the last part of the third missionary journey. From Miletus, Paul and his friends sailed in a coastal ship to Cos, a distance of about 45 miles. The next day they journeyed to Rhodes, which was about 75 miles to the east. Rhodes was a famous city-state. After spending the night, the missionaries continued, probably in the same coastal ship, to Patara, about 70 miles distant.

There the travelers found a larger ship bound for Phoenicia, some 400 miles away. During the journey, they passed by the island of Cyprus, which probably brought back memories of the first missionary journey. Eventually, they reached the busy port of Tyre. After seven days there, they sailed on to Ptolemais and from there to Caesarea. They traveled the rest of the way to Jerusalem on foot. That trip required at least two, probably three, days.

Reasons for Avoiding Jerusalem

In Tyre, Paul and his friends sought out the Christians of the city (Acts 21:4). They had a great time of fellowship with them. When the time came for the missionary group to leave, all of the believers, including wives and children, accompanied them to the seashore. Together they knelt and prayed. Then they reluctantly said good-bye to each other.

91

Warning in Tyre. But while the missionaries were in Tyre, the believers "told Paul through the Spirit not to go up to Jerusalem" (Acts 21:4). Paul, nevertheless, remained steadfast in his conviction that the Spirit was leading him to Jerusalem and eventually to Rome. We'll see later that the message of the believers and Paul's conviction were not necessarily contradictory.

In Ptolemais, Paul and his friends enjoyed a day of fellowship with the believers. Notice how Paul sought the company of fellow Christians. When we truly love and serve God, we long for contact with the people of God and find help in that communion.

Warning in Caesarea. When the group arrived in Caesarea, they lodged in the home of Philip, the evangelist. We last heard of him in Acts 8:40 (about 20 years earlier). Philip now had four virgin daughters who served the Lord with him. They "prophesied," which I take to mean that they had a special gift of foretelling the future and of declaring scriptural truth in that context. No doubt both the guests and the hosts received great benefit from this contact. The sacred record informs us that they remained together "many days" (21:10).

During this period, a prophet named Agabus joined the company, having arrived from Judea. No doubt he is the same person mentioned in Acts 11:28, where he predicted the coming of a great famine. Now Agabus delivered another prophecy, this one related specifically to Paul. He dramatized the message from the Holy Spirit by taking Paul's belt and tying his own hands and feet with it. The prophets of the Old Testament regularly illustrated their prophecies from the

Lord (see Isa. 20:2-4; Jer. 13:1-11; 27:2-8; Ezek. 4; 5; 12:1-6; I Kings 13:1-5; Isa. 12:1-6).

Agabus then warned, "So shall the Jews at Jerusalem bind the man who owns this belt, and deliver him into the hands of the Gentiles" (Acts 21:11). Then everyone in Philip's home pleaded with Paul not to go up to Jerusalem.

Reason for Going to Jerusalem

Paul didn't agree with the majority opinion of his friends. He agreed that both the believers in Tyre and Agabus had received the right message from the Holy Spirit. He knew that suffering and imprisonment awaited him in Jerusalem and farther on. But Paul and his friends reached very different conclusions.

Let's follow the reasoning. His friends said, "Paul, suffering awaits you in Jerusalem. You should avoid this difficulty. Therefore, don't go to Jerusalem." But Paul said, in essence, "I know that suffering lies ahead in Jerusalem. But I will not be sidetracked. God is leading me to Jerusalem."

Paul spoke strongly to his friends: "What do you mean by weeping and breaking my heart [literally— weakening my resolve]? For I am ready not only to be bound, but also to die at Jerusalem for the name of the Lord Jesus" (Acts 21:13).

Did a stubborn streak keep Paul from accepting the advice of his friends? I don't think so. Paul had demonstrated great perseverance in the work of God. (There's a fine line between perseverance and stubbornness, isn't there?) But he also exhibited sensitivity to God's guidance. Think of his experience when he wanted to preach in Asia and Bithynia (16:6-10). The Holy Spirit directed him to Macedonia. Paul went where the Holy Spirit guided.

Paul determined he must go to Jerusalem, even though he had to go against a strong current of Christian love and consideration for him. Do I think Paul was infallible and always made the right decision? No. In fact, I know he wasn't. No one but God is infallible. However, in this particular case, I feel strongly that Paul was right and that he was following the will of God when he insisted on going to Jerusalem. I think some of his friends finally understood this, too, because they said, "The will of the Lord be done" (21:14).

Even today, well-meaning Christians may try to steer us away from God's will out of concern for our safety and comfort. Some folks still feel that dangers and difficulties indicate a wrong decision. Such thinking does not find support in the Scriptures. Remember what Paul and Barnabas told the new converts: "We must through many tribulations enter the kingdom of God" (14:22).

Difficult Choice of Adaptation

Some of the disciples from Caesarea indicated their support of Paul by going with him to Jerusalem (Acts 21:16). Furthermore, they made preparations so that Paul would receive the necessary hospitality in Jerusalem. They made contact with Mnason of Cyprus. We know very little about this man. We do know that he made himself available at the right time. He exercised the grace of hospitality when Jerusalem was very crowded and lodging would be hard to find. As many as two million people packed into Jerusalem at that season.

Reception of Paul

Many Christians in Jerusalem welcomed Paul and his party gladly. Acts 21:17 implies that a reception committee cordially greeted Paul when he arrived at Mnason's home.

The next day, Paul had a more formal meeting with James and the elders of the church. He reported in detail what God had done among the Gentiles through his ministry. The whole group glorified the Lord when they heard the good news.

Recommendation to Paul

The elders then informed Paul about a serious problem they were facing. "Many myriads of Jews" had believed (Acts 21:20). That was good news! But a large number of them were "zealous for the law" (v. 20). In other words, they insisted passionately on keeping the Old Testament ritual.

The problem was that the Judaizers were actively circulating the rumor that Paul was teaching the Jews "to forsake Moses, saying that they ought not to circumcise their children nor to walk according to the customs" (v. 21). Paul, of course, did nothing of the kind. He had circumcised Timothy, because Timothy was half Jewish (16:3). Paul had even taken a Nazarite vow, according to Jewish custom (18:18).

The elders had a recommendation for Paul. He should join four men who had taken a Nazarite vow. He should be purified with them. Then everybody would know that he kept the Law and that the reports about him were not true.

The elders quickly pointed out that they did not require these rituals of the Gentiles. They were respecting the decision of the Jerusalem Council. However, we get the feeling that these church leaders were yielding too much to the fanatical Judaizers, who were dominating the Jerusalem scene.

Response of Paul

This recommendation placed Paul in a dilemma. Without a doubt it bothered him to see how strongly the Judaizers were influencing the thinking of the elders. Still, he loved his Jewish brothers and would go to great lengths to help them spiritually.

Paul decided to accept the recommendation of the elders. He was willing to adapt. He joined the four other men in their vow (Acts 21:26).

Did Paul do the right thing? Many Bible students think that he had the right motive but that he made a big mistake. I agree. Furthermore, it is evident that the greater fault lay at the feet of the Jerusalem elders. False rumors about a person like Paul would not be silenced by some compromising action. They should have met these falsehoods head-on and marshaled the facts to show that Paul was not rejecting Jewish custom and ritual.

Next, the same rumormongers who had sought to blacken Paul's reputation added still another falsehood to their list. Some Jews from Asia had seen Paul in the city with Trophimus, an Ephesian. Paul's adversaries accused Paul of having taken Trophimus into the temple (vv. 28,29). According to Jewish Law, no Gentile was permitted to enter the temple. A Gentile could visit the Court of the Gentiles, but entering the temple itself could bring the death penalty. So the fanatical Judaizers were charging Paul with one of the worst violations of Jewish Law. Even though he was preeminently a missionary to the Gentiles, Paul's record of consideration for his Jewish background made the accusation totally absurd. But the gullible crowd accepted this horrible lie as a fact.

May God help us not to fall into the trap of "supposing" and reaching unjust conclusions! A Christian must always base his actions on truth. Even when he speaks, it must be with truth spoken in love.

Riot Against Paul

Paul's desire to adapt led to disaster. He accepted the recommendation of compromise, thinking he was not abandoning his convictions. But the plan backfired. Gullible people believed the scandalous accusations of the Asian Jews. "All the city was disturbed" (Acts 21:30). The angry mob seized Paul and dragged him out of the temple. Some of the temple guards immediately shut the temple doors so that the Holy Place would not be defiled by fighting. The crowd was at the point of killing Paul.

A question kept battering my mind as I reviewed this passage. Where were the elders who had encouraged Paul to take the vow? Where were the "many myriads of Jews" who had believed? The Bible implies that they were conspicuous by their absence. They did not raise their voices in protest. They abandoned Paul.

While fellow believers didn't come to the rescue, Roman soldiers did. The commander of Jerusalem's garrison, composed of 1000 soldiers and quartered near the temple at the Fortress of Antonia, immediately marshaled his centurions and soldiers to restore order. When the crowd saw the soldiers coming, "they stopped beating Paul" (v. 32). Strangely, the commander first bound Paul with chains and then afterward asked who he was and what he had done. He received such confusing answers from the mob that he gave orders to take Paul to the barracks. When they reached the stairs, the multitude became so infuriated that the soldiers had to lift Paul above the crowd to keep him from being torn apart. His enemies kept yelling, "Away with him!" (v. 36). Recall that the crowd cried out against the Lord Jesus in the same way (Luke 23:18).

Request of Paul

Paul then made an unusual request in the Greek language. He said to the commander, "May I speak to you?" (Acts 21:37). With great surprise the commander replied, "Can you speak Greek?" (v. 37). Up to that moment the commander mistakenly believed that Paul was an Egyptian rebel. History informs us that the Egyptian in question had led an uprising against Rome. He had marched with a large force to the Mount of Olives to overpower the Roman garrison and seize Jerusalem. He had promised his followers that, at his word, the walls of Jerusalem would fall (which didn't happen). The Roman forces defeated the Egyptian and his army. But he didn't give up easily. He escaped and led a force of assassins who constantly carried daggers under their cloaks. They did not hesitate to use them when opportunities arose.

Paul made it plain that he was not the Egyptian. He was a Jew who came from the important city of Tarsus. Paul said to the commander, "Permit me to speak to the people" (v. 39). The chiliarch (Greek word for an officer over 1000 men) granted his permission.

Paul motioned with his hand for the people to be silent. Then he spoke to them in Hebrew. Even though he was the victim of mob action, he still acted with authority and power—the power of the Holy Spirit. In the next chapter, we'll examine Paul's speeches to the mob and to the Sanhedrin. When this whole tumult ended, the Lord appeared to Paul in a vision to cheer, commend and commission him (23:11).

Paul was no doubt discouraged. Had he done the wrong thing? Why had so much trouble resulted? But down deep he had the assurance that he was following the will of God. He reminds me of Martin Luther. Good friends urged Luther not to risk the danger of going to Worms. But he replied, "Though there were as many devils in Worms as there are tiles on the housetops, yet will I go thither." When we have our orders from the Lord, we can go forward as true disciples, following Him.

Chapter 9

Paul's Good Defense
(Acts 22:1—23:11)

We saw clearly in the last chapter that great danger surrounded Paul in the hands of the angry mob. We also observed his Christian courage in asking permission to speak to the crowd. These events, however, must have shaken him severely. He was a man, with a nature just like ours. Nevertheless, Paul knew where to turn for the resources he did not possess. The Lord would not fail him.

Before the Mob

Paul addressed the mob in Hebrew. When they heard him speaking in that language, they became silent (Acts 22:2).

He Described His Former Conduct

Once more we see how diplomatically Paul sought common ground with his adversaries. He reminded the group of his Jewish heritage. He had been born into a strictly Jewish background in the city of Tarsus. He had learned about the Law at the feet of Gamaliel. He had a zeal for God, as many of them did. In fact, he was so zealous he had become a leader in opposing the followers of Jesus. He succeeded in throwing many of them—both men and women—into prison. He even received permission from the high priest and council of elders to go to Damascus and bring believers from there to Jerusalem in chains.

He Recounted His Conversion

Paul then told the mob about the event that changed the direction of his life. Jesus Christ appeared to him on that road to Damascus. Those who accompanied him saw the great light but didn't hear the One who was speaking to him. The Lord Jesus said, "Saul, Saul, why are you persecuting Me?" (Acts 22:7). Paul replied, "Who are You, Lord?" and Jesus answered, "I am Jesus of Nazareth, whom you are persecuting" (v. 8).

Paul then asked, as many others have, "What shall I do, Lord?" (v. 10). The Lord told him to go into Damascus, where he would receive full instruction concerning what he should do.

The light had blinded Paul, so he had to be led into Damascus. There God had prepared a man named Ananias. He helped restore Paul's sight. As a result of these events, Paul believed, was baptized and rejoiced in the forgiveness of his sins.

He Explained His Commission

Paul proceeded to explain how the Lord had guided him. First, Ananias instructed him concerning his future service. Ananias said to Paul, "You will be His witness to all men of what you have seen and heard" (Acts 22:15).

God later on confirmed the commission to Paul. He said, "Depart, for I will send you far from here [Jerusalem] to the Gentiles" (v. 21). In the years that followed, Paul steadfastly carried out that commission.

He Caused a Great Reaction

Paul's reference to Gentiles struck the Judaizers with the force of a shotgun. When he spoke that word, they exploded like dynamite. They even cried out, "Away with such a fellow from the earth, for he is not fit to live!" (Acts 22:22). They kept on screaming in their rage. They even tore off their clothes and threw dust into the air. What a tragic scene!

Before the Officers

Once again the Roman soldiers stepped in to protect Paul. However, the commander ordered him to be examined under scourging. Scourging was a terrible thing. The person was tied by wrists and feet to a pole in such a position that the whipping would do its greatest damage. The whip was made of thongs with bits of metal and bone imbedded in them. Scourging often resulted in the death of the victim or in permanent injury to him.

We can understand, therefore, why Paul appealed to his Roman citizenship. He asked the centurion, "Is it lawful for you to scourge a man who is a Roman, and uncondemned?" (Acts 22:25). Paul was not only saving his own skin but also that of the military officers. Since it was illegal to scourge a Roman citizen, the commander and his men could easily have lost their positions—and maybe even their lives—over this incident.

The commander then personally interviewed Paul. While the commander had purchased his Roman citizenship, Paul could say, "I was born a citizen" (v. 28). He had the right to ask for correct legal treatment.

Immediately, the situation changed. I can imagine the Roman officers scurrying around to undo what they had begun. They quickly untied Paul. They put the whip out of sight. It was obvious that the commander was afraid because of what he had done to Paul.

Before the Sanhedrin

The next day the soldiers removed all of Paul's bonds (Acts 22:30). The commander had decided to take Paul before the Sanhedrin, hoping to learn the reason for the accusations against him.

His Conflict With the High Priest

Paul began his defense before the religious council with a very positive statement: "Men and brethren, I have lived in all good conscience before God until this day" (Acts 23:1). This irritated Ananias, the high priest, who gave the command to strike Paul in the face. (This is not the same Ananias as found in Acts 22.)

Paul vigorously rebuked Ananias, "God will strike you, you whitewashed wall!" (23:3).

His Courtesy to the High Priest

Paul received a rebuke in return. Members of the Sanhedrin asked, "Do you revile God's high priest?"

(Acts 23:4). Paul then replied courteously, "I did not know, brethren, that he was the high priest; for it is written, 'You shall not speak evil of the ruler of your people' " (v. 5). He was quoting Exodus 22:28.

This incident raises a question. Did Paul really not know that Ananias was the high priest? He probably didn't know for three reasons:

1. The Sanhedrin was no doubt in an informal session. In that case the high priest would not sit in the center, apart from the others. Neither would he wear his high priestly vestments.

2. Paul had not spent much time in Jerusalem since his conversion. He would not know who was filling the office of high priest.

3. If Paul had poor eyesight, he might not have been able to discern who was the high priest.

Paul immediately expressed regret for having spoken as he did. He had respect for the office, though he would find it difficult to respect Ananias as a person. Ananias was serving as an interim high priest. He had a tainted reputation as a glutton, a rapacious robber and a quisling in Roman service. In A.D. 66, when war broke out against Rome, he was dragged by the Jewish fighters from an aqueduct where he was hiding. The insurgents put him to death along with his brother Hezekiah.

Paul sought to act like a Christian gentleman. He would not stoop to conduct similar to that of the unworthy high priest. What about you and me? Do we conduct ourselves like Christians, even when others treat us in an unchristian manner?

Although Paul did not approve of what the Pharisees believed and practiced, he had more in common with them than with the Sadducees. The Pharisees believed in the resurrection and in angels. The Sadducees believed in neither.

Paul saw an opportunity to give testimony to his faith. He said, "I am a Pharisee, the son of a Pharisee; concerning the hope and resurrection of the dead I am being judged!" (Acts 23:6). He was certainly telling the truth. He had gone everywhere with the message that Jesus had not only suffered and died but had also risen from the dead. Therefore, all Christians had the hope of resurrection and endless life.

Paul's declaration set the Pharisees and Sadducees against each other. In fact, the Pharisees began to defend Paul, saying, "We find no evil in this man" (v. 9).

The opposing parties exploded into such great dissension that it looked like they might pull Paul to pieces. Consequently, the military commander ordered his soldiers once again to surround Paul, remove him by force and bring him safely to the barracks.

Before the Lord

At this point Paul could have been greatly discouraged. It looked as if everything had gone wrong. He had faced three very violent situations—at the hands of the Judaizer mob, at the orders of the military men and before the religious council. Why had all this happened? Had he missed the will of God?

Paul did not need to defend himself before the Lord.

105

Instead, the Lord defended and reassured him. The night following the ordeal with the Sanhedrin, God spoke to Paul with great assurance (Acts 23:11). The promise he received contained three important elements.

The Lord Cheered Him

Paul heard the words, "Be of good cheer" (Acts 23:11). No doubt he had experienced low moments following the vicious attacks upon him. This would be most natural. But the trusting Christian receives resources that are supernatural. In the darkest moments, he can hear the great promise: Be of good cheer. The presence and power of his Lord dispels the darkness. "The Lord is my light and my salvation; whom shall I fear? The Lord is the strength of my life; of whom shall I be afraid?" (Ps. 27:1).

The Lord Commended Him

"As you have testified for Me in Jerusalem" (Acts 23:11). Things had not gone well in Jerusalem. Paul could have believed that he had failed. But the Lord's evaluation revealed that Paul had given a proper testimony. He could rest in the fact that God was satisfied. That's all Paul needed to know.

The Lord Commissioned Him

"So you must also bear witness at Rome" (Acts 23:11). Paul could take heart in knowing that the Lord planned to empower him for further service. He had longed to go to Rome. Now he knew that God planned to send him there to testify of God's love and salvation.

Although many circumstances were negative, Paul was reassured that he was moving positively, according to the divine plan.

Our great God still encourages His children in times of special need. If we live in close fellowship with Him through Jesus Christ, then we, too, shall receive His cheer, His commendation and His commission.

Chapter 10

God Leads His Dear Servant Along
(Acts 23:12—24:27)

Psalm 37:12,13 affirms, "The wicked plots against the just, and gnashes at him with his teeth. The Lord laughs at him, for He sees that his day is coming." Here in Acts 23:12,13 we see Paul's enemies plotting against him. But God laughs at them and foils their plot. In verse 11 the Lord had encouraged Paul with a great promise. Now He is carrying out that promise step by step.

Plot Against Paul

More than 40 Jews banded together to kill Paul. They took an oath that they would neither eat nor drink until they had murdered him. In reporting their oath to the chief priests and elders, they used very strong language. They literally said, "With a curse have we cursed ourselves" (Acts 23:14).

After reading the whole story, I wonder what these men did when their plan failed. If they had kept their oath, they would have died of thirst and starvation.

These fanatics had a clever plan. They wanted the chief priests and elders to ask the commander to bring

Paul before the council again. They were to pretend that they wanted to learn more about Paul. Then, while the soldiers were en route to the council, the Jews would attack by surprise and quickly kill Paul.

We get an idea of the ferocity and hatred of these men when we realize that their plan, though clever, involved great danger. The Roman soldiers would strongly repel the attack, and a number of the would-be assassins would no doubt lose their lives.

It appears that the high priests and elders liked the idea. Scripture says nothing about their rejecting the plan.

Providence to the Rescue

Paul's enemies thought no one else knew the secret of their diabolical plan. However, in God's providence, one of Paul's relatives somehow discovered what they were proposing to do.

Presence of a Nephew

This is the only time in Acts that we find a member of Paul's family mentioned. We surmise that his nephew had come to Jerusalem to study or to attend the Feast. We don't know if he divulged the secret because he was a believer in the Lord Jesus or because of kinship ties. We don't even know how he discovered the plot. We do know that God had this nephew in the right place at the right time. His presence was not coincidental—it was providential.

Paul's nephew immediately informed his uncle about the proposed ambush (Acts 23:16). Paul, in turn, called for one of the centurions and urged him to take the young man to the commander. The commander cordially received the nephew, took him aside privately and asked, "What is it that you have to tell me?" (v. 19).

Paul's relative told the whole story to the commander and urged him not to allow Paul to go before the council. The commander instructed the young man not to tell anyone that he had discovered the secret and alerted the military.

In all these details we see the certain guidance of our sovereign Lord. For example, the readiness of the commander to accept the report of the young man shows God at work in this situation.

Provision of a Military Escort

The commander acted immediately to thwart the intentions of Paul's enemies. He ordered his men to prepare a strong military contingent to take Paul safely to Caesarea (Acts 23:23,24). The force consisted of 200 infantry, 70 cavalry and 200 spearmen—a total of 470 soldiers.

Notice this interesting touch—the commander made sure that Paul, a prisoner, would have a mount to ride on (v. 24). Instead of being murdered by his opponents, Paul traveled in style and in safety to Caesarea.

The convoy left that night at 9:00 p.m. They traveled through the night until they reached Antipatris, a distance of about 35 miles. From there, the 70 horsemen continued on to Caesarea, while the other 400 soldiers prepared to return to Jerusalem. For the first part of the journey, they needed extra protection because of the roughness of the road and the presence of many Jews. From Antipatris to Caesarea (a distance of about 25 miles), the road leveled out and the escorts moved through an area of more Gentiles than Jews.

Presentation to the Procurator

Felix was the procurator, or governor, of Judea. As such, he had authority over Jerusalem. Therefore, the commander, Claudius Lysias, sent Paul to him to be judged by him. He also wrote a letter to Felix, which was delivered by his soldiers along with Paul.

The letter of Claudius Lysias presented Paul in a favorable light. The commander told Felix that he saw nothing charged against Paul that would merit chains or death. The entire account reveals that Claudius had positive feelings toward Paul. I believe this was true for two reasons. First, God was working in the commander's heart. Second, Paul's conduct and reaction to his circumstances must have impressed him greatly.

Paul Before the Procurator

Felix governed Judea from A.D. 52 to A.D. 59. He was born a slave but later became a freedman, just like his brother Pallas. However, Felix quickly forgot about his humble beginnings. He married three different princesses in succession. His second wife, Drusilla, was the daughter of Herod Agrippa I and the sister of Herod Agrippa II and Bernice.

Tacitus, a historian, said that Felix exercised the power of a king with the mind of a slave. Felix had the reputation of being a mean, profligate, cruel ruler. He was finally removed from being procurator because of the bloody way in which he handled civil strife between Jewish and Gentile inhabitants of Caesarea.

False Accusations of the Enemies

After five days, Ananias (the high priest) and the elders came to Caesarea to accuse Paul (Acts 24:1). They brought with them an orator-lawyer by the name of Tertullus. He began his speech with a good deal of flattery for Felix, even though everyone knew that the compliments were false.

Next, Tertullus explained the charges against Paul. He called Paul a plague, or a pestilence. He made three specific accusations. First, he called Paul an insurrectionist (v. 5). In other words, he was a person who incited civil disorder. That was a serious accusation, because the Roman rulers dealt harshly with those guilty of sedition. Second, Tertullus charged Paul with being the ringleader of the Nazarene sect (v. 5). Third, he maintained that Paul tried to profane the temple (v. 6). Compare this with Acts 21:28, where his enemies accused Paul of defiling the Holy Place. Now they had reduced the charge to "trying to profane the temple."

Firm Answer of Paul

Notice how beautifully Paul answered Tertullus. First, he addressed Felix courteously but without flattery. Next, he firmly denied the accusations of insurrection and profaning the temple. He made it plain that his enemies couldn't prove their charges. He reminded

112

the court that those who claimed he had defiled the temple should have brought some evidence.

Then Paul admitted some positive things. He worshiped God according to "the Way." His enemies called this a sect. But Paul showed how "the Way" was just a fulfillment of what was written in the Law and the Prophets. He believed in the resurrection of the just and the unjust, just as some of his accusers did.

It's inspiring to see how firmly and clearly Paul refuted the charges against him. He gave his testimony with confidence. Paul had received great help from the Lord's visit to him in the night and from the promises God had given him (Acts 23:11).

Notice that Paul stated why he had come to Jerusalem—to bring "alms and offerings to my nation" (24:17). These offerings had been collected from the Gentiles, who gratefully gave to help the poor saints in Jerusalem and Judea. Rather than being opposed to the Jews, Paul and the Gentiles loved them and sought their welfare.

Foolish Action of Felix

After hearing all the evidence, Felix should have set his prisoner free. Instead, he dodged the real issue by saying, "When Lysias the commander comes down, I will make a decision on your case" (Acts 24:22). All the while, Felix knew that Lysias had no plan for coming down. He had already sent Felix a letter stating his position—Paul had done nothing to merit death or imprisonment. The best we can say for Felix at this point is that he treated his prisoner with consideration. He gave him much liberty. He allowed Paul's friends to

113

visit him and provide for his needs. But those measures fell far short of the acquittal Paul deserved.

Procurator Before Paul

Felix sat as judge at Paul's trial. Actually, he was on trial much more than Paul was. Felix appeared to be a free man, but he was really enslaved to his wicked life. Paul was imprisoned, but he was really free through faith in Christ. He enjoyed the glorious liberty of a son of God.

The Message He Heard

It's strange but true that Felix and Drusilla wanted to speak with Paul (Acts 24:24). Though living corruptly, they must have had some deep-seated longings to live virtuously, as Paul did. His fervency for God and his commitment to the Gospel must have impressed them.

Paul didn't waste his time and theirs by talking about the weather or the time of day. He reasoned about righteousness, self-control and the coming judgment. What a contrast! Paul spoke of righteousness to a man known for being unjust. He reasoned about self-control to a couple who had followed the way of intemperance. He talked about judgment to a man who usually thought he was above being judged.

The Mercy He Spurned

Felix was afraid (Acts 24:25). Some translations say he "was terrified." The emotions of the procurator were shaken. A struggle was going on in his soul. The Lord was inviting him, through Paul, to accept the offer of salvation in Jesus Christ. But in that crisis moment he refused to yield. He procrastinated. He answered, "Go away for now; when I have a convenient time I will call for you" (v. 25). An Indian proverb declares, "To say tomorrow is to say never."

Commenting on this scene, Alexander Maclaren said eloquently, "Do not delay, because delay is decision in the wrong way; do not delay, because there is no reason for delay; do not delay, because delay robs you of a large blessing; do not delay, because delay lays up for you, if ever you come back, bitter memories; do not delay, because delay may end in death" (*Expositions of Holy Scripture*, p. 298).

The Money He Sought

Not only did Felix postpone a decision to accept the Lord's message, he also sought a bribe from Paul (Acts 24:26). Possibly Felix thought that, since Paul brought offerings to Jerusalem, he had an abundance of personal funds at his disposal.

Felix often called Paul to come and converse with him. No doubt Paul was a stimulating conversationalist. However, Felix kept on thinking that Paul might offer him a large sum of money to gain his favor. But Paul had no intention of buying his freedom. He longed to see Felix forgiven by God through faith in Christ. Sad to say, Felix no longer demonstrated the interest in spiritual matters he once had. By ignoring the voice of his conscience and the call of God, his heart became progressively hardened. Contact with the fervent apostle no longer made a noticeable impact on the heart and spirit of Felix.

115

The Mistake He Made

Instead of acting justly, Felix sought the favor of the Jews (Acts 24:27). He should have released Paul, but he was more interested in advancing his political fortunes. How shortsighted he was! Not only did Porcius Festus succeed Felix as governor of Judea, but Felix also started on a downward slide. He disappeared from public notice. He was fortunate to escape with his life. He passed from history with a reputation for intrigue, cruelty and immorality. What a tragic story! Felix had his day of opportunity, but he turned his back on God. As far as we know, he continued on that course to the end of his life.

What a contrast is found in the life of Paul! His outward circumstances didn't look very favorable. But the Lord's approval rested on him. Though bound, he was free. During this waiting time, he was being prepared for the demands and opportunities that lay ahead. He kept on hearing the Lord's promise: "Be of good cheer" (23:11).

Today, all over the world, fellow Christians are enduring persecution and imprisonment. Many are gaining the martyr's crown. In their trials they are experiencing the Lord's promises and presence. I have met and talked with many of these brothers and sisters. Their testimonies have thrilled me.

We, too, can draw on the Lord's resources. The same Lord Jesus who stood by Paul will stand by us. Let's trust Him—and find His answers for the challenges of life today. God still leads His dear servants along.

Chapter 11

Paul's Good Confession
(Acts 25:1—26:32)

We show our true character by how we speak and act in contrary circumstances. In chapter 4 we saw a great illustration of that as we witnessed Paul and Silas praying and praising at midnight in the Philippian jail (Acts 16:25). They were so filled with the joy of the Lord that when they were rudely bumped (like a cup), their joy overflowed.

In Acts 25 and 26 we will see another illustration of how a true servant of the Lord Jesus can shine in adverse conditions. Paul, as a prisoner, gave a good confession because he continued to believe and to rest in the Lord's promises. Let's look at some important elements in his confession.

His Courtesy

We have seen it before and now see it again—Paul treated the corrupt officials courteously. They must have tried his patience. The Jewish authorities especially leveled false charges against him. Yet, he continued to conduct himself as a genuine gentleman. The shady lives of Felix and Herod Agrippa II did not inspire respect, yet Paul treated them with respect because of the offices they held.

117

We have learned how evil Ananias, the high priest, was. Felix, the procurator, also had a very tainted reputation. Festus was a better person than either of them; yet he, too, was more interested in gaining favor than in administering justice. He freely admitted that he had no valid charges against Paul (Acts 25:26,27). Nevertheless, he did not set Paul free.

And what shall we say about Herod Agrippa II, the last of the Herods? His great-grandfather had murdered the innocent children in Bethlehem at the time of Jesus' birth. His great-uncle had ordered the execution of John the Baptist. His father had killed James and planned to kill Peter (12:1-4). Agrippa II was living with his sister Bernice. He and other family members lived in open sin. They loved to bask in their limited power and did so with great ostentation (25:23).

Even though these people did not deserve respect, Paul treated them courteously. When he gave his confession before Agrippa II, he publicly acknowledged that the king was an expert regarding the customs and questions concerning the Jews (26:3). He spoke whatever good he could about the king.

Why did Paul act so kindly to these unworthy people? First, he believed that Christians should be subject to the governing authorities (see Rom. 13:1,2). Second, he accepted this principle: "Repay no one evil for evil" (12:17). Third, he desired by testimony and conduct to lead men and women to faith in the Lord Jesus Christ.

We should observe Paul's example very carefully. The message of the cross is inherently offensive to the unsaved person (see Gal. 5:11; I Cor. 1:18,23). But we

118

should not be offensive in our presentation of the Gospel or in our treatment of those who need salvation (see Phil. 1:10).

His Conviction

Paul's testimony rang with conviction. We learned earlier that Paul reasoned with Felix and Drusilla about righteousness, self-control and the coming judgment (Acts 24:25). He spoke so fervently and convincingly that Felix was terrified and asked him to leave. The earnestness with which Paul delivered his message convicted him.

The same thing happened as Paul gave his confession before Festus and Agrippa II. Paul's intensity and his penetrating message bothered Festus. He yelled, "Paul, you are beside yourself! Much learning is driving you mad!" (26:24). Festus was mistaken. In reality, he was the one beside himself. Paul, on the other hand, was in his right mind.

A few verses later we see how intent Paul was as he spoke with King Agrippa II about matters of eternal importance (vv. 26-28). Paul genuinely believed the message he was presenting and the testimony he was giving. He, therefore, spoke with deep conviction.

Good confession is always characterized by intense conviction. We should not be lukewarm or half-hearted as we share the Gospel. When the Holy Spirit fills us, He sets us on fire. Even when others mock us, such opposition does not intimidate us because the Lord gives us the boldness to speak fervently in His name. More people would listen to our message if they

119

saw that its truth gripped us so strongly that we had to speak with conviction.

One day a prison chaplain in England was speaking with a convicted criminal about the Gospel. After hearing the message, the prisoner said, "Padre, if I believed that, I would crawl across England on broken glass to tell men and women about it."

Paul spoke with that kind of conviction. His message impacted those who heard him. We, too, should believe and treasure God's message so much that others can see our fervency when we speak. As we yield to the Holy Spirit, He will give us the words to express His truth. Then He will inject our speech with His power to convict our hearers and to lead them to repentance.

His Concentration

We can learn a great deal from the content of Paul's confession. He focused on foundational truths. He didn't wander into unimportant detours. It will help us to look specifically at the great beliefs Paul brought into his testimony.

First, Paul referred to the promises God gave to the Jews (Acts 26:6,7). More specifically, he mentioned the hope that "God raises the dead" (v. 8). He returned to the same theme in verse 22 when he said, "I stand, witnessing both to small and great, saying no other things than those which the prophets and Moses said would come." Consistently and effectively, Paul pressed home the point that the message of the Gospel was the fulfillment of God's promises given to the Jews over many years through His prophets.

In verse 23 Paul again underlined the truth he had been proclaiming to everyone everywhere: "That the Christ would suffer, that He would be the first to rise from the dead, and would proclaim light to the Jewish people and to the Gentiles."

We can witness effectively when we focus on the great themes of the Gospel. We need to concentrate on the basics. We should avoid a fruitless discussion of nonessential matters.

Paul then combined his presentation of foundational truths with a personal testimony. He related how these doctrines and the Person of Christ had affected his life. Personal testimony shared in connection with basic beliefs is very powerful.

Paul enthusiastically recounted the story of his conversion. He freely confessed how wrong he had been to persecute the followers of the Lord Jesus. But he also emphasized the grace of the Lord in calling him away from the wrong road into His service. I can imagine how his eyes must have sparkled as he said, "Therefore, King Agrippa, I was not disobedient to the heavenly vision" (v. 19).

I'm convinced that we should share our personal testimonies more than we do in witnessing to unbelievers. Our testimony might not be as dramatic as Paul's. Nevertheless, we should have something to share about how the Lord brought us to Himself and how He has blessed our lives since then. If we don't have something current to share, we need to reestablish fellowship with our Lord so we can speak from fresh experience of His goodness.

His Compassion

Paul was giving his witness as a prisoner. He could have been very concerned about his own predicament. He had appealed to Caesar and did not know what the outcome of his trial would be. However, he enjoyed so much of the Lord's peace that he had a genuine concern for his captors and judges.

Revealed in His Invitation to Agrippa

Notice how directly he addressed King Agrippa and pressed home a personal application: "King Agrippa, do you believe the prophets? I know that you do believe" (Acts 26:27).

A great deal of discussion has revolved around Agrippa's reply (v. 28). His response is difficult to translate. The New International Version renders it: "Do you think that in such a short time you can persuade me to be a Christian?" The Williams translation says, "In brief you are trying to persuade me and make a Christian of me!" Another possible version is "You think, it would seem, to make me a Christian very easily."

I was interested to see Alexander Maclaren's paraphrase of Herod's reply. He suggests that the king was really saying, " 'And do you really suppose that it is so easy a matter to turn me—the great Me, a Herod, a king,' and he might have added, a sensual bad man, 'into a Christian?' " (*Expositions of Holy Scripture*, pp. 326,327).

It's obvious that Paul's message and manner made a deep impression on Herod. Yet we do not see any evidence that he was ready to leave his sinful life and to receive Jesus Christ by faith.

Reinforced by His Statement of Concern

Paul's feeling of compassion reached its climax in his statement recorded in Acts 26:29: "I would to God that not only you, but also all who hear me today, might become both almost and altogether such as I am, except for these chains." We find nothing of resentment in Paul's impassioned plea. He wasn't feeling sorry for himself. He longed for the people to whom he was speaking to find wonderful freedom in Christ. They were prisoners of their sins. Although he was bound by chains, he was free in Christ. Therefore, he could show real compassion—even to those who were keeping him in chains when he had done nothing worthy of punishment.

Once more we have a great example to follow. May God grant us such compassion and love for others, even when we must give our testimony under difficult conditions. This makes me recall the beautiful words of Toña, an Auca believer who was killed by his own people. He had gone to the fourth and most isolated group of Aucas to give them the Gospel and to share his own testimony of salvation. For six weeks these people listened to his witness. Then, inexplicably, they speared him to death. As he lay dying, Toña said, "I love you and God loves you. Jesus came a long way to bring you salvation. I came a long way to tell you about Him. I love you and God loves you." That demonstration of concern by a dying Christian moved the hearts of his assassins. Not long after the incident, those

123

misguided people came out of their jungle seclusion and sought contact with other Aucas who had already believed. Now some Aucas in group four are followers of Christ.

God can give us this kind of care and compassion. As we yield to the Holy Spirit, He will pour the love of God into our hearts (Rom. 5:5). Then, needy people around us will benefit from the overflow. It's true that the Book of Acts does not tell us that Festus, Bernice and Herod came to faith in Christ. But Paul had faithfully given them God's message and had shown them the love of Christ. I'm sure that as others in the room heard his vibrant testimony and saw Christian love in action, a seed was planted in their hearts that resulted in salvation for some of them.

Chapter 12

On the Way to Rome
(Acts 27:1—28:10)

Luke's account of the journey to Rome as told in Acts 27 and part of 28 is a "classic" and a "masterpiece." I recommend that you read it carefully a number of times on successive days. I also suggest that you consult the maps at the back of your Bible or obtain a Bible encyclopedia and trace the course Paul and the others sailed. I had never realized as fully as I do now that the worst force of the storm hit the travelers out on the open water. That must have been some experience!

The Start of the Journey

We are told that Paul was delivered, along with some other prisoners, to Julius, a centurion of the Augustan Regiment (Acts 27:1). This was probably a special regiment that had the responsibility of serving as messengers for imperial military business.

Julius appears in a very favorable light in Luke's account. It's interesting to see how regularly centurions are mentioned in a positive way in the New Testament. Julius is no exception. When the ship docked at Sidon, "Julius treated Paul kindly and gave

125

him liberty to go to his friends and receive care" (v. 3). It must have encouraged Paul greatly to have fellowship with his Christian friends and to receive their ministry to him.

Later in the story, when the ship was wrecked off the shore of Malta, the soldiers wanted to kill the prisoners for fear that they would escape (v. 42). But this considerate centurion "wanting to save Paul, kept them from their purpose" (v. 43).

Not only did Paul enjoy the kind treatment of the centurion; he was also blessed with the help of two faithful companions, Luke and Aristarchus. Luke, of course, accompanied Paul on a great part of his missionary journeys. Now he had joined Paul for this trip to Rome. We first met Aristarchus in Acts 19:29 where he was seized by the mob during the uproar in Ephesus. He is mentioned again in Colossians 4:10 as a fellow prisoner with Paul and in Philemon 1:24 as a fellow laborer with Paul.

These men probably offered to accept the condition of prisoners so that they could be with Paul. Their companionship must have refreshed Paul repeatedly on the long journey to Rome. Still today the ministry of believers to fellow believers in need is a very significant and precious part of Christian service.

The first part of the long voyage to Rome ended at the port of Myra. "There the centurion found an Alexandrian ship sailing to Italy, and he put us on board" (Acts 27:6). This was probably a larger ship with a cargo of grain (see v. 38), since Egypt provided a good deal of grain for Rome and adjoining communities.

The trip from that point on became increasingly

difficult, but they did reach Fair Havens on the island of Crete without mishap (vv. 7,8). There Paul advised the pilot, the owner and the centurion that if they tried to press on at that time of the year, they would be inviting disaster. Sailing in that part of the world was dangerous between September and November. After that, it was impossible until March. The Fast (or Day of Atonement) had passed, which meant they had already entered the month of October.

In spite of the advice of Paul, a seasoned traveler, they decided to try to reach Phoenix, near the western end of Crete. It offered better facilities for wintering than Fair Havens did. So the centurion yielded to the opinion of the pilot and owner. The majority of the passengers and crew agreed with that decision.

The Storm

Everything looked very favorable at first. Because a south wind was blowing softly, the group put out to sea and sailed close by Crete (Acts 27:13). Then suddenly the situation changed. A tempestuous, gale-force wind assaulted the ship. It wasn't possible to head into the wind, so the crew decided to let the ship be driven by the furious northeaster. They experienced temporary relief under the shelter of an island called Clauda. They took advantage of that reprieve to haul the trailing service boat on board. The crew needed help from the passengers for this task, for Luke says, "We secured the skiff with difficulty" (v. 16).

The next 14 days turned out to be a nightmare for those on board. They "were exceedingly tempest-tossed" (v. 18). "Neither sun nor stars appeared for

127

many days" (v. 20). No small tempest beat on them (v. 20). They "were driven up and down in the Adriatic Sea" (v. 27).

Try to imagine the scene: tossed about on the open sea, loose objects flying to and from different parts of the ship, many passengers seasick and vomiting.

Many joined in the heroic efforts to save the ship. They wrapped strong ropes or cables around the ship to hold it together. The next day, they lightened the vessel by throwing all unnecessary objects overboard. On the third day, even the passengers helped to throw the ship's equipment and furniture overboard (v. 19). Eventually they went so far as to get rid of all the cargo (v. 38).

We aren't surprised to read: "All hope that we would be saved was finally given up" (v. 20). The occupants of the ship abstained from eating—and we can understand why. It looked as if everything was hopeless.

The Steadfastness of Paul

In the midst of the terror and confusion, at least one man was experiencing peace and calm—Paul. The tempest on the outside had not entered his soul. He called for courage: "Paul stood in the midst of them and said. . . . 'I urge you to take heart, for there will be no loss of life among you, but only of the ship' " (Acts 27:21,22). Before giving them that encouragement, however, he reminded them all that they should have listened to him when he urged them not to sail from Crete (v. 21).

How could Paul have such great calm during such a terrible storm? We learn the secret of his confidence in

128

the next sentence he spoke: "For there stood by me this night an angel of the God to whom I belong and whom I serve, saying, 'Do not be afraid, Paul; you must be brought before Caesar; and indeed God has granted you all those who sail with you' " (vv. 23,24).

Paul experienced peace because he knew without any doubt that he was God's child. Even the storm could not change that fact. The angel had reminded him that he belonged to his Lord. Furthermore, Paul had confidence in the Lord's declared purposes. God had promised that Paul would bear witness in Rome. It looked momentarily as if the tempest would change all that. But storms do not thwart God's purposes. He controls the seas and the winds. Paul, therefore, could have complete confidence because he was God's possession and was moving by God's purpose.

Paul added a confirming note: "I believe God that it will be just as it was told me" (v. 25). As a child of God, we can declare, "God said it. I believe it. That settles it," for "all the promises of God in Him [Jesus Christ] are Yes, and in Him Amen, to the glory of God through us" (II Cor. 1:20).

Several elements in this story reveal Paul's loving care and concern for his fellow passengers. First, we see how he foiled the attempt of the crew members to abandon the ship. Their help would be needed if all of the passengers were to reach shore safely, so Paul told the centurion, "Unless these men stay in the ship, you cannot be saved" (Acts 27:31). The centurion responded by ordering the soldiers to cut away the ropes and let the skiff fall off. The skiff was lost, but the crew remained on board to help when the ship ran aground.

Second, Paul urged all on board to take nourishment (vv. 33,34). They were weakened through abstinence from food and the strain of the storm. They would need extra strength to survive. Paul set the example by taking bread, giving thanks to God for it, breaking it and beginning to eat. This encouraged his fellow passengers, and they, too, ate.

I love this story. Paul's steadfastness in the storm sets a great example for each of us. The doomed and desperate passengers took heart when they saw his trust. He conveyed the message to them that God—not the wind or sea—was in control. In our most disheartening circumstances, we can testify of our Lord and say by word and action, "I believe God."

The Shipwreck

The sailors planned to guide the ship before the wind with the hope of beaching it on the island that lay before them (Acts 27:39). If they succeeded, passengers and crew would arrive on land safely without further difficulty.

However, they encountered an unexpected obstacle. Where two seas met, they ran aground on a sandbar. The prow stuck fast in the soil, but the stern was battered by the waves, and the ship began to break up.

The soldiers wanted to kill the prisoners, fearing that some of them might swim away (v. 42). We can understand their concern because, in the Roman system, a guard who let a prisoner escape had to suffer the prisoner's punishment.

The centurion nixed the plan of the soldiers. He was

especially concerned that Paul's life be spared. It's significant to see the centurion's interest in Paul. He had observed his conduct. He quickly realized that Paul was an unusual prisoner. We can only imagine what continuing effect Paul's testimony had on this outstanding centurion.

This part of the story ended exactly as Paul had predicted. The ship was lost—but all the passengers were spared. Some swam to land; others used boards and broken pieces of the ship to float to shore. "And so it was that they all escaped safely to land" (v. 44). The shipwreck had a happy ending in spite of the unexpected grounding and in spite of the soldiers' plan.

The Stay on Malta

The survivors learned that they had landed on the island of Malta (may be Melita on your map). The islanders provided very good hospitality. They "showed us unusual kindness" (Acts 28:2). They soon had a fire going to warm the chilled passengers, for it was rainy and cold. The leading citizen of the island, Publius, received the group and entertained them courteously for three days (v. 7).

Once more the story focuses on Paul. We see him gathering sticks for the fire. Great people don't mind doing humble tasks. As W. Graham Scroggie observed, "The Church's greatest theologian gathers sticks for the fire" (*The Acts of the Apostles*, p. 184).

While Paul was collecting the wood, a viper came out because of the heat and fastened on his hand. The natives immediately concluded that Paul was a murderer whom justice was pursuing. To their great sur-

131

prise he shook the snake off his hand into the fire and suffered no ill effects. The natives quickly changed their opinion and now declared that he was a god.

While Publius was entertaining the group, Paul learned that the father of this hospitable man was ill with fever and dysentery. Paul prayed for him, laid his hands on him and healed him. The news about this miraculous healing spread quickly. People came from all over the island seeking help. The language used in verse 9 implies that they were cured, not only miraculously but also by normal medical means. No doubt Luke, because he was a physician, attended many of the sick people. If that was the case, then we have the first example of medical missionary service.

The experience on the island of Malta began in a pleasant way. It ended in the same manner. The islanders honored the travelers in many ways. No doubt they appreciated the medical attention they had received from Paul and Luke. The people of Malta honored the passengers in a very practical way by giving them the equipment and provisions necessary to continue their journey. In other words, they helped replace what had been lost in the shipwreck.

Looking back over this story, we see God's care and control in circumstances that seemed out of control. Even more than Paul's steadfastness, we see the faithfulness of the Lord whom Paul served. Because our Lord is the same yesterday, today and forever, we can trust Him fully, just as Paul did.

Chapter 13

Bearing Witness at Rome
(Acts 28:11-31)

In Acts 23:11 the Lord assured Paul that he would bear witness at Rome. Two events threatened that promise. First, Paul's enemies developed a plot to assassinate him. But their plan was discovered, and the Roman military took decisive action to protect Paul. Second, on the voyage toward Rome, the ship carrying Paul and 275 other people encountered a violent storm. Shipwreck resulted, but all lives were spared. God was keeping His promise to lead Paul to Rome.

Encouragement From Christian Brothers

After the passengers had spent some time on the island of Malta, Paul and his group boarded an Alexandrian ship that had wintered there (Acts 28:11). This ship had on its prow the figures of the Twin Brothers—Castor and Pollux—who were two of the favorite gods of seafarers. This part of the trip went much more smoothly than the first half. The travelers first reached Syracuse, the most important city of Sicily. They remained there three days. Because the wind was not

133

entirely favorable, they followed a circuitous route before arriving at Rhegium, an important harbor in the south of Italy. Then a better south wind blew, and they quickly covered the distance of about 180 miles between Rhegium and Puteoli, the chief port of Rome. Puteoli lay about 140 miles southeast of Rome.

At Puteoli

The Lord continued to prepare Paul for his witness at Rome. In Puteoli he found fellow believers who received him and his friends happily and extended them Christian hospitality. They enjoyed fellowship for an entire week (Acts 28:14). Some commentators think that Julius, the centurion, had important business in Puteoli and, therefore, chose to remain for seven days in that port. In that case verse 14 would be better translated: "We found brethren and were cheered among them, remaining seven days." Other commentators feel that the centurion did a special favor for Paul in arranging this stopover of seven days. If that was the case, such action would indicate the centurion's growing respect for Paul.

Whatever the reason for the delay in Puteoli, Paul and his friends must have benefited greatly from this contact with the Italian Christians. I believe strongly that the Lord arranged this meeting to prepare Paul for the ministry that lay ahead.

At Appii Forum and Three Inns

From Puteoli the travelers set out on foot for Rome. Imagine Paul's surprise and delight when, at a distance of about 45 miles from Rome, a number of Christian friends met him and his partners at a place called the Appii Forum. They had heard Paul was coming, and they came to meet him. Ten miles closer to Rome, at Three Inns, still more believers joined the group. As they walked together, they must have talked joyfully about God's blessings and their Christian experience. These friends had taken the time and effort to travel that distance so they could encourage and cheer Paul.

Acts 28:15 informs us that Paul "thanked God and took courage." Once more we see how the Lord was preparing and fortifying Paul for the witness he would give in Rome. When the Lord calls us to a specific service, He promises to provide the necessary resources. Not only does this story speak of God's provision, but we also see how important it is for believers to encourage each other in the Lord's work. The fellowship of the Christians in Puteoli and the kindness of the believers who came to meet Paul certainly refreshed him and his friends.

Entrusted With Special Privileges

Paul, along with the others, finally arrived at Rome. That city was, of course, the great center of the Roman Empire. About two million people resided there—one million of which were slaves. Those who were not slaves included 700 senators, 10,000 knights (who occupied public positions) and 15,000 soldiers. The vast majority of the rest were paupers. The history of that time tells us that they lived for "bread and circus"—that is, to have sufficient food and to be entertained.

135

Note what the centurion did when the group arrived in Rome. He "delivered the prisoners to the captain of the guard" (Acts 28:16). These individuals were no doubt kept in the ordinary prison facilities to await trial. "But Paul was permitted to dwell by himself with the soldier who guarded him" (v. 16). The centurion and the soldiers whom he commanded had acquired a great appreciation for Paul. They must have been convinced by this time of Paul's innocence. Surely the centurion must have given Paul a good recommendation and influenced the decision to allow Paul to have "his own rented house" (v. 30).

Think about how this arrangement contributed to Paul's opportunities for witness. Inquirers could have private conferences with him. Even the Roman soldiers were exposed to Paul's preaching and teaching, since he was always guarded. Guard changes meant that more men heard Paul's message. It must have had a great impact on them.

We don't know how Paul paid the rent on his house. Perhaps he received offerings from friends in various churches. Or he might have worked at his tent-making trade once again.

The liberty Paul enjoyed made it possible for his friends to visit him and to work with him. Timothy often was with him (Phil. 1:1; Col. 1:1; Philem. 1:1). Sometimes Tychicus was present (Eph. 6:21), as was Epaphroditus (Phil. 4:18). Also present were Aristarchus, Mark, Justus, Epaphras, Luke and Demas (Col. 4:10-14). Paul's conduct and ministry served as a great example for his friends. On the other hand, their presence must have strengthened Paul and contributed to his overall witness.

Having Liberty to Speak

The last seven words of Acts inform us that Paul had great liberty for preaching and teaching during his two years as prisoner in Rome (Acts 28:31). I believe God ordered these circumstances because it was His purpose for Paul to have this opportunity for witness. The Lord can give an open door for service, even when the circumstances seem completely contrary. Even prisons become pulpits under God's direction!

Illustrations abound in our time of the open doors God gives His servants, not only when liberty abounds but also when liberties are restricted. I can think of a Chinese preacher who has had many rights of citizenship taken from him, including the right to travel. But this has not limited his ministry. People come to him from all over the country to be taught. And cassette tapes of his teaching are scattered far and wide throughout the land.

The Lord arranged for Paul to have great liberty for carrying on a very fruitful ministry. In other situations the Lord still provides an open door, even when ordinary freedoms are canceled. If we recognize our need, keep His Word and do not deny His name, He promises to set before us an open door (see Rev. 3:7,8).

Exhortation to Leaders of the Jews

Paul continued to have a great burden for the Jews, his kinsmen according to the flesh (see Rom. 9:1-5). In

137

fact, after arriving in Rome, he waited only three days before he called the leaders of the Jews together (Acts 28:17). Alexander Maclaren pointed out that this speedy action gives us another illustration of Paul's diligence and persistence. Then Maclaren remarked, "What a long holiday some of us would think we had earned, if we had come through what Paul had encountered since he left Caesarea!" (*Expositions of Holy Scripture,* p. 377). No doubt, those three days were not spent resting. They would have been filled with contacts with Roman Christians and details connected with coming to his new residence.

His Explanation of the Facts

Paul quickly explained the facts of his imprisonment to them. Once more he affirmed that he had done nothing wrong. He reported that the Roman rulers had found no cause for punishing him. They would have freed him, but the Jews continued to press their case against him. Finally, he felt he had to appeal to Caesar. But he made it clear that he was not accusing his nation (Acts 28:19).

Then Paul pressed home his recurring theme. He was a prisoner "for the hope of Israel" (v. 20). His enemies accused him of wrong doctrines when he was, in fact, proclaiming the hope toward which Israel had looked for centuries—the hope of the Messiah. That hope had found its fulfillment in Jesus Christ, who died and rose again.

Their Excuses

At this point, the Jewish leaders refused to commit themselves. It was no doubt true that they had not

138

received letters or personal messengers with last-minute reports concerning Paul. But I doubt that their expressions of ignorance were true. In one way or another, news of what had happened in Jerusalem and Caesarea must have reached them, since Paul had been a prisoner in Caesarea for at least two years.

Although they professed ignorance concerning the controversy surrounding Paul, they nevertheless revealed their prejudice by saying, "For concerning this sect, we know that it is spoken against everywhere" (Acts 28:22). They did indicate, however, that they would like to hear Paul's thoughts on the matter.

His Emphasis on the Kingdom and Jesus

The Jews chose a day for further discussion. Many came to Paul's house at the appointed time. When Paul spoke, he concentrated especially on the kingdom of God and on Jesus, the King of that kingdom. He used the Old Testament to show how the Law and the Prophets pointed forward to the Lord Jesus. He earnestly sought to persuade them from morning till evening (Acts 28:23).

Their Expression of Belief and Disbelief

"Some were persuaded by the things which were spoken, and some disbelieved" (Acts 28:24). The Jews couldn't agree among themselves about Paul's message. In fact, after they had departed, they continued to dispute among themselves (v. 29). We are encouraged to see that some of the Jews believed. A portion of the seed Paul was sowing fell on good ground.

Before the Jewish leaders departed, Paul reprimanded them by using Isaiah 6:9,10. This passage gives the picture of hearts that are fat, or thick, and therefore unfeeling; of ears that are heavy, or dull, and consequently unheeding; and of eyes that are smeared over and, as a result, incapable of opening.

Ever Extending the Gospel

The last two verses of Acts show Paul fervently carrying on his ministry in Jesus' name. Luke informs us that he "received all who came to him" (Acts 28:30). I'm sure the word quickly spread about this unusual prisoner. Many came to see and hear Paul. Some probably sought him out of curiosity. Others arrived with sincere questions—like Onesimus, who was wonderfully converted (Philem 1:10).

Paul not only stood ready to receive each one who came, he was also ready to preach and teach. Verse 31 makes it clear that he was both evangelizing with the Gospel and also teaching those who wished to go forward in the Christian life.

At the same time that he was ministering in person, he also had a ministry through writing letters. It is generally agreed that Paul wrote Ephesians, Philippians, Colossians and Philemon during this imprisonment. These books inform us that Paul had a most fruitful ministry during these two years.

We naturally wonder why Luke didn't tell us what happened beyond these two years. Some think he planned to write another book. But that isn't the fundamental reason why Acts ends as it does. Luke didn't write Acts to give us the life history of Paul. He wrote the book to tell us about the ongoing ministry of Jesus

Christ through the Holy Spirit. The resurrection activity of the Lord Jesus led to the establishing, equipping and extending of the Church. Acts ends like an unfinished book because the great work of reaching out with the Gospel wasn't finished. It still goes on today.

I vividly remember the shining face of the Chinese preacher I met who had suffered great persecution. As he told me about the present triumphs of the Gospel in his land, he said to me, "Brother, here in China we are writing the 29th chapter of Acts." God calls us to the same glorious task that occupied the time and energy of the early Christians. Counting on the Lord's help, may we do our part with the same fervor and power of the Holy Spirit they demonstrated!

Paul's example still challenges us today. Our last glimpse of him shows him serving his Lord with a burning heart. Tradition tells us that he suffered martyrdom in A.D. 67. No doubt, he kept sharing the message of the Lord Jesus as long as he had opportunity. He finished his course. He kept the faith. We can do the same in Jesus' name and by the power of His Spirit.

Bibliography

Barclay, William. *The Acts of the Apostles,* rev. ed.; (*The Daily Study Bible Series.*) Philadelphia: The Westminster Press, 1976.

Bruce, F. F. *The Book of the Acts.* (*The New International Commentary on the New Testament.*) Grand Rapids: Wm. B. Eerdmans Publishing Co., 1954.

LaSor, William Sanford. *Church Alive.* Glendale, California: Regal Books, 1972.

Maclaren, Alexander. *Acts 13—Romans.* Vol. 12 of *Expositions of Holy Scripture.* 17 vols. Grand Rapids: Baker Book House, 1982.

Morgan, G. Campbell. *The Acts of the Apostles.* Old Tappan, NJ: Fleming H. Revell Company, 1924.

Scroggie, W. Graham. *The Acts of the Apostles.* (*Study Hour Commentaries.*) Grand Rapids: Zondervan Publishing House, 1976.

Walker, Thomas. *Acts of the Apostles.* (*Kregel Expository Commentary Series.*) Grand Rapids: Kregel Publications, 1965.

Back to the Bible is a nonprofit ministry dedicated to Bible teaching, evangelism and edification of Christians worldwide.

If we may assist you in knowing more about Christ and the Christian life, please write to us without obligation:

Back to the Bible
P.O. Box 82808
Lincoln, NE 68501